Single, Sexy &

SEXLESS

A Guide To
Maximize
Your Single
Life

DAPHNE R BEARD

Dedication

      I dedicate this body of work to a virtuous woman of great grace, class, and purity. A woman whom I have witnessed endure life's most challenging events yet remain faithful to her God and selfless to her family. One who is resilient and lives an integral life before God and man. To my own personal Superwoman and greatest supporter, my mother, Daphne Woodard-Beard. Thank you for always staying true to who you are and Whose you are. Thank you for giving me life and making sure it was filled with faith, love, and unending support. I love you always!

-Your first born & your forever "Minnie Rose."

Contents

Preface

At the time of writing this book, I, the author, am currently and intentionally single for several reasons. First, God made it clear to me that I needed to enter a season of aloneness where He could download to me some truths I will need before marriage. Secondly, I felt strongly that, in order to be as effective as possible, I needed to be free from all bias and/or emotional distractions that could potentially persuade my most honest understandings as God has given them to me. Thirdly, I am on the "All-Counterfeits-Ask-Her-for-a-Date" list from which I am hoping to be banned. The handsome members of that list waste your mental space, cute outfits, and new makeup. On a serious note, a wealth of knowledge can be learned from every experience we have. The laughs, the tears and even the moments of rolling of your eyes until the white parts show all have profound lessons to teach you.

Now, despite its title, this book is quite helpful, and dare I say useful, for single, courting and engaged women. These pages will offer several opportunities to confront toxic single life perspectives and discover new approaches to obtaining healing and wholeness. This book also undertakes a journey to discover what "sexy" really means and to explore some uneasy truths underneath our female sexuality. Taking this journey will include examining past and present experiences that have inadvertently influenced our future sexual selves.

Additionally, we will delve into what is considered practically taboo in many of today's churches but so well-explained in the media—sexual desire and sexual sin—will be addressed. Finally, a very practical, yet Biblical, approach to living a sexless life in our modern sexually desensitized society will also be explored. These issues will get real, so if you were born "under the pew," you may have to take a few breaths before continuing in some of the sections. As a young, Christian woman who chooses to practice abstinence until marriage, I believe firmly – the more knowledge of truth we possess, the less likely Christians will fall subject to living as slaves to sin. In Hosea 4:6A, God states, "My people are destroyed for lack of knowledge." In the original Hebrew, the word "destroyed" means to cease or perish and "knowledge" means understanding or skill. In essence, God said His own people die because they do not possess understanding. It is my belief that the opposite is also true – Gods people unequivocally thrive when they obtain, own, and operate in knowledge. It is my sincere prayer that you, the appreciated reader will be provoked in thought, challenged in lifestyle and fulfilled in spirit.

A Prayer for My Sisters

Dear Merciful Father,

I thank You for every one of Your daughters who will read this book. It was not by accident that it happened to fall into each one's hands, but God, You predestined it to be so before the foundation of the world. You strategically assigned this material to them because You are calling them higher in their relationship with You. Today, individually and collectively, we give our whole selves to You. Take our bodies and purify them with Your Word. Cause our flesh to die and fill us with your precious Holy Spirit. Cleanse our hearts from desires that are contrary to Your Word. Renew our minds today. Take out inappropriate thoughts, sinful lust, perverted flashbacks, painful memories, and anything that would distract us from thinking on those things that are pure, holy and of good report.

Today we cast down vain imaginations and every high thing that exalts itself against the knowledge of God, and we bring every thought into obedience to Christ. We plead the blood of Jesus over all generational curses over us, our children, and our children's children. We realize we cannot live a holy life unto You in our own strength, so empower us by the power of the Holy Spirit. Let us be sensitive to Your voice and take the way of escape that You provide for us in times of temptation.

We declare that Christ is Lord over our lives, and we will not render ourselves to another. Whether single, engaged, courting, or married, help us to trust You in every aspect of our lives. We thank You for the opportunity to live a life rendered unto You. We praise You for the endless benefits attached to our obedience to Your Word.

In Jesus' name, Amen.

Introduction

My mother often tells me a story about when she was giving birth to me. She made a declaration based on the excruciating labor pains she was experiencing. She declared, "God, if You will get me out of this, I will never be back here again."

Well, my mother faithfully upheld that declaration for nearly eleven years—until God blessed our family with my younger brother followed by my younger sister less than two years later. The nearly eleven-year-baby boycott was the result of an unforgettable, painful experience. My mother's response to the excruciating labor pains mimic the world-renowned physicist, Isaac Newton's third law of motion that states "for every action there is an equal or opposite reaction."[1] Without delving into a deep scientific explanation of interacting objects and forces, simply put every reaction a human being makes is the product of a previous action that has taken place in their life.

Our response to the world around us is based on our own personal experiences. Experience has a way of gifting us with some of life's most precious jewels when we are open to learn what God intends to teach us. To those who have ears to hear, experience has a voice that offers truths in the good, the bad and the ugly.

Besides the Holy Spirit Himself, experience has been one of my greatest teachers of all time. It has taught me to own my truths at all cost, to bear the burden of my mistakes and to benefit from the gifts of wisdom and growth. God has freed me from some hard-to-shake habits and has given me great peace to share my not-so-pretty experiences in the hope of setting women all over this world free from the masks of shame, guilt and fear that we all have voluntarily or involuntarily worn. I promised God that if He freed me, I would take my mask off and tell my story.

I must say, it has been extremely liberating to own my mistakes and to no longer be owned by them. Now that I am *mask-less* (I made that word up; just go with it), I have come to realize that I really love the woman I am becoming. Without the pains of my past and the preparation of my present, I would in no way be able to reap the fruit of my future. My goal is to empower women to conquer past wounds, acknowledge present worth and live above mediocrity in the future.

Confession: I am a lover of God's Word and the truth that is infused into all sixty-six books. In truth we are set free from shallow senses of who society wants us to be. Truth is good for the soul but can sometimes be a hard pill to swallow. With that being said, I admonish you not to run away in those moments when you may feel resistance toward hard truths being addressed. In those moments likely, God is speaking specifically to the part of you that resists true wholeness in God alone. Be sure to pray and ask God to show you what in you is rejecting the truths of His Word. Then, ask Him to open your heart to consider something new.

I also must admit that I am a bit of a revolutionary. I absolutely despise being put in a box; I dread being compared to people or fitting stereotypes. Unapologetically, I was raised to be myself. So, with all of these preliminaries in mind, put on your seatbelt because some unpopular concepts will be encountered in the hopes of breaking the silent shackles that hold so many women hostage. When we are held hostage, we are denied privileges that should be offered to us. Do you know how many women live their entire lives being denied privileges that should be afforded to them? Truth is a privilege that so many die without experiencing because lie serum is easier to swallow—even when completely unaware.

Prior to beginning this book, I encourage every reader to pray earnestly that God would prepare your heart, mind and spirit to receive what He has specifically included in this read for you. May you uncover every vital tool necessary to maximize your single life journey!

I - *Single*

Are you really single?

The term "single" for the purpose of this read will be used to

refer to unmarried individuals. Countless women who state, claim, and

scream they are single really are not single at all. Some are more involved

than married women. I hope you still have your seatbelt on because we

are about to go *there*. Too often, we women mistake aloneness for

singleness. Just because you are unmarried, not dating or have no one

who sleeps with you at night does not make you single. Being without a

physical partner does not make you any more single than sitting in a fish

tank would make you a fish. What makes you single is simplicity. Let us

go deeper.

The Greek word *aphelotes* is used in Scripture to mean

"singleness." This same word translates to *simplicity*, which is "the state of being uncomplicated or being easy to understand or do." [2] With regard

for the initial definition, unless your single life is uncomplicated or easy

to understand or do, you are not single—God's way, that is. It is possible

to be physically single while emotionally married or spiritually divorced.

A great number of single women believe they have "moved on" from past

relationships but are still emotionally tied to former lovers. Such

attachments include cycles of comparing every man that follows to the

one who preceded. Others have been subject to failed relationships of

which they blame God for resulting in spiritual divorce. This occurs

when single women who initially sought God prior to the relationship

stop seeking Him after the relationship. Their prayer time decreases or

becomes non-existent, fasting turns into a thing of the past. Church

services, Bible study or any form of ministry participation is no longer a

part of their weekly rotation. When the natural relationship fails, they

indirectly or directly blame God. They develop the desire to manage their

future affairs on their own terms rather than asking God to intervene.

They may include God in other areas of their life, but their personal life

becomes off-limits. This split or distance between them and God grows

as they become increasingly self-willed. In time, they refrain from

seeking Him thus consciously or unconsciously filing for spiritual

divorce. Have you ever filed for spiritual divorce? If so, now would be an ideal time to repent or turn away from the God-less dating space you are in. It is not by chance that you are reading this part and feeling convicted or sorrowful – that is the Holy Spirit's way of lovingly nudging you to turn back to God. He alone is the sole, primary factor to help you maximize your single life. Without Him, any information offered here will be of little to no effect as it will only be temporary. You need Him so that which you learn and apply can result in true, lasting transformation. You have sought family, friends, men, and even skilled experts – it is time to allow the Creator of all access to your personal life again. If you are not sure about how to do so, begin by saying this prayer aloud:

"Heavenly Father,

I come to You humbly acknowledging I have allowed my own will to supersede Yours. I confess I have selfishly and anxiously sought after my own fulfillment rather than Your plan for my life. I confess I tried dating without You which resulted in a spiritual divorce from You including heartbreak, regret, and emptiness. I confess I have felt angry at You and knowingly or unknowingly blamed You for my single life woes. I repent (turn) from selfishness, pride and/or _____ (insert as is fitting for you.) 1 John 1:9 says, "If we confess our sins, (You) are faithful and just to forgive us our sins, and to cleanse us from all unrighteousness." I ask You to forgive me and help me resist the temptation to live any part of my life without You. Take charge of my single life and intervene in my dating life as I surrender all matters of my personal life to You. Thank You for forgiving me and granting me a fresh start in Jesus' name. Amen."

Now, let us further interact with our opening question: Are you really single? The Bible makes two references to *"singleness in heart"* between masters and servants. In both cases, Ephesians 6:5 and Colossians 3:22, obedience was the ultimate goal. This suggests that a tell-tail characteristic of true singleness is obedience to God. My earnest belief is that when a woman is truly single, her ability to obey God increases. She becomes more sensitive to His leading and less influenced by her own. Each day, her ability to submit to His will for her life becomes more realistic and simplistic. A single woman whose life is centered around obedience to God will experience an increased longing to be in right standing with Him. In addition to a decreased desire to go astray or make decisions outside of the will of God.

If your single life is not simplistic or uncomplicated, you should take inventory of your obedience to God. Ezekiel chapter 11 reveals God gave His people "singleness of heart", so they were able to walk in His statutes and keep His ordinances. Simply put, He gives them a heart for Himself so they may obey Him. Possessing a heart for God, as depicted in that same chapter means relinquishing the stony heart of the flesh. This means, women who desire simplicity in their single life must be willing to release their current heart of stone. What if I told you the only thing standing between the bitter you and the better you is your ability to release? When you choose to release your bitter, bruised, or broken heart – you make space for goodness and peace. This means, the presence of complications, aggravations and frustrations become of little to no effect. It goes without saying that you cannot control external factors however you can control your internal responses. It has become contagiously popular to say a single woman is waiting on God. However, I would like to challenge that theory by suggesting that the opposite can also be true. Simply put, God is waiting on you. When you are a child of God, He takes great, tender care of you and does not want you to live with a heavy heart. With that in mind, I believe God has a better, new heart for you and He is waiting for you to release the bitter heart of old. Having a heart for God is key in truly being single. Some single women are physically single but emotionally entangled as their hearts beat for everything and everyone else except God. A heart for God means you take on His burden and His yoke which Matthew 11:30 states, are easy and light. Some single women fail to have a heart for God because we have barriers that prevent us from truly being single. Now let us consider three that are quite common: progress interruptions, voids and false closure.

Progress Interruptions

A few years ago, I left a toxic relationship filled with innumerable red flags I chose to bypass because we had history. Side note – not all history is healthy history. Simply because you have spent years or even decades with an individual does not mean those years were beneficial to your overall well-being. The end of this seemingly life-long, drama-filled saga hit me like a ton of bricks. I was left with the heavy weight of betrayal coupled with the dread of deception. Feeling as if actual steam seeped out of both of my ears; I spent months infuriated. Rather than taking time to explore those difficult emotions, I opted to focus on my career. Going above and beyond at my place of employment allowed me to receive a promotion, accolades and yes, more money! The latter allowed me to pay off my car note early and move into a beautiful luxury apartment in an ideal neighborhood with much more space than I needed. For you single sisters, like myself, who absolutely love your heels, you will appreciate this next statement – my apartment had four fabulous walk-in closets! My "heel babies" and I were living the dream. At last, it felt like the air I breathed was lighter. Life as I knew it had become stress-free, easy going and purely simple. After spending years enduring the polluted air of that toxic relationship, I developed a newfound appreciation for that which was fresh. Mentally, I concluded that the increased progress was the result of my decision to walk away.

However, along with every new triumph in life comes a new temptation. After approximately six months post-breakup, I made a new male friend that seemed to appear out of nowhere. He had a great listening ear, was easy to talk to and offered supportive advice on coping with the loss of my previous relationship. Many single sisters would agree, the presence of a male is helpful when endeavoring to better understand the male perspective. Without being a romantic interest, a sincere male friend can be quite beneficial during your single life journey. Word to the wise: be sure to know their intention and be clear on your own. Overtime, I unknowingly replaced my former relationship with the new friendship. His keen ability to make me laugh enabled me lose sight of the anger I felt from my previous relationship. We spent countless occasions sharing meals, telling jokes, and creating "insiders." Allowing him into my emotional space had much greater implications than I realized or was prepared for. Eventually, I noticed a change in him in that he would become upset when I mentioned going out on a date which led to confusion surrounding whether or not we were in a relationship. What I once considered a friendship had evolved into a gray "situationship." Meaning, unlike every other relationship I had been in – this one had no title, no clarity and ultimately no point. When I realized I was entertaining a well-adjusted bachelor who had no desire to mature beyond his bachelor pad mentality, I ended it. I felt hurt after leaving him and quickly realized I failed to process the initial hurt (which was concealed by anger) from the first broken relationship.

As single women, we can easily ignore our inner hurt by honing into the outer anger that serves as a coverup. Why do we do this? I believe it is easier to be angry than it is to confront the hurt. It takes a level of vulnerability that we resist opening ourselves up to especially after doing so was the very reason we were hurt to begin with. If letting our guard down and allowing someone into our emotional space left us hurt, the very last thing we want to do is allow ourselves to feel vulnerable again. Instead, we choose anger as a defense mechanism to avoid going beyond the surface level of our emotional pain. Another reason we choose anger or any other emotion over hurt is to avoid self-analysis. If we only focus on what "he" did that hurt us, it keeps us in the clear of dealing with our own shortcomings. If I had taken the necessary time to acknowledge and process my hurt, I would not have settled for a "situationship." As single women, how many times do we ignore the hurt and cling to the superficial? No matter how hard we cling, in time, we are met with what we fought so hard to escape– the difficult, unpleasant feeling of hurt. We must confront our hurt and every challenging emotion to experience the simplicity of single life. Being single or living in "the state of being uncomplicated" is much more than being unmarried. It is both the benefit and burden of detaching from anything and anyone who enhances obstacles to pursue simplicity at all costs. True singleness is attained after one endures the pains of earnest reflection that in time brings forth healing.

Deciding to live a simplistic single life can sometimes appear as if an alarm has gone off in the earth that informs all the wrong ones to take notice of you. This makes it of the utmost importance for women to evaluate who is in their life that could slow down their progress. Anyone or anything that is able to interrupt the presence of your simplicity diminishes your efforts of truly being single. Now, my dear sisters, I know some of them may wear the best-smelling cologne, drive the most stylish cars and appear to have all their ducks in a row; however, if they add complications to your single life, they are an interruption. Once you identify who they are, dismiss them. Yes, you read it correctly: dismiss them. You may not be able to physically remove them (if you work with or go to the same gym), but you can mentally dismiss them and emotionally evict them. Consider this, the longer you allow them to pause or slow down your momentum, the more you delay your own progress. Not to mention, you may prevent those who are connected to your progress from advancing.

Whether or not you realize it, not everyone is willing to help you progress. Progress interruptions give you the opportunity to choose who you will allow in your life and who absolutely cannot be a part of it. Even those who you have helped progress may not be so moved to help you do the same. You will come to find out some people only wanted you to do better—but not better than they thought you could do and certainly not better than them. People can limit the amount and impact of your success if you allow them to. Therefore, it is imperative to break free from those who cannot handle your progression. Sometimes, the person can be your closest girlfriend who is accustomed to hearing you complain about how miserable your last relationship was that she cannot accept how joyous your present one is. Watch for those who only have a listening ear for your pain but turn a deaf ear to your progression. Single sisters, free yourself from anyone who claps when you cry and cries when you clap. Read that again. These individuals serve as agents of counterproductivity, a subtle yet blatant tool of the enemy. One that appears to prevent you from moving backwards while simultaneously stifling you from moving forward. Biblically speaking, Judas Iscariot, for instance, appeared to help carry Christ's mission forward by working alongside Him in ministry. However, inwardly and ultimately outwardly attempted to stifle His mission from progressing by turning Christ in to the religious leaders. Be mindful of those who have a mission to stop or slow down your progress.

Be sure to surround yourself with those who are likeminded. Being around others who are progressing can give you the motivation you need in difficult times. Contrary to popular belief, progress does not always result in a positive feeling. Instead, it can sometimes make you feel as though you have so much further to go which blinds you from how far you have already come. Hence why you need likeminded people around you who will speak life to you when you feel as though your progress is in vain. Once again, I ask you: Are you really single? If you have been stopped or stifled by progress interruptions that have caused your single life to become anything but simplistic, you may not be. Let us consider two additional factors that can strip one of their true singleness: voids and false closure.

Voids

It goes without saying, whenever a relationship that you were emotionally invested in ends, you experience some sort of emotion. Whether sadness, anger, loneliness, happiness, or relief—a plethora of emotions are deeply felt. Regardless as to how long the relationship lasted, the significant memories of special places and favorite activities can sometimes become a source of regret or resentment. During such times, many single women have a sense that something is missing. There is often a longing for mental, emotional, spiritual, or physical stimulation that was once present. This longing creates a void and a desire to fill it which results in a new, insignificant relationship.

Our default setting easily allows us to place another man in that space without realizing he is not able to fill it. When we have a void, we have need to be made whole. Truth is, only God can fill a void as He is the only One who makes us whole. When we fill a void with people or things, we only suppress it. On the other hand, when we fill a void with God, we overcome it. The truth of the matter is a woman who is whole *in a relationship* will be whole after the relationship is over because her wholeness did not depend on a man but was rooted in God. After a breakup, you are vulnerable which makes it the perfect time to seek God. Psalm 34:18 says, *"The LORD is near to those to those who have a broken heart and saves such as have a contrite spirit."* When you are broken before God, He is near to you and takes pleasure in making you whole again. If you want a void truly filled, draw closer to Him through prayer, meditation and studying of His word.

False Closure

Deleting his phone number, blocking him on social media and trashing every couple photo you own does not mean you are over him. Wondering how I know? I have been there. I did all of those things as well as threw out every gift my ex had ever bought me only to find myself pondering over a laundry list of "what-if's." Years after one breakup, I found myself in this place of questioning because I had a false sense of closure. I thought that because I no longer talked to him nor saw him that I was over him. But the subtle mention of his name in conversation would cause my mind to wonder about all of the possibilities—like, *did I ruin something that should have been forever? Was my unwanted single life my punishment for missing "the one"?* Um, no. Not quite. Let me share a brief glimpse into this story...

I was twenty years old, still in college and had fallen out of love with my first love. I decided to really give my entire life to Jesus. I only wanted to focus on Him which, at the time, meant I wanted to stay as far away from sin as possible. During that time, my first love had given his life to Jesus and had reconnected with me. He wanted us to date again; I declined. As time passed, he eventually shared with me that God told him I was going to be his wife.

I shared with him I would have to pray about the situation as God did not tell me what He claimed He told him. I never actually prayed about it. I only said I would because I was not ready for that sort of commitment. I was finally becoming consistent in being committed to God; there was no way I was going to take on another huge responsibility—especially not at twenty years old. I was not mature enough at the time to even consider being a wife. During that time, I had three dreams that I was going to marry another person. When I shared these dreams with my first love, he was completely broken. He stopped speaking to me, left church and in time went back to the street life he was accustomed to before Christ. I felt such guilt and sadness, so in a sense, I mourned.

I then tried to pursue a relationship with the person whom I thought I was supposed to marry based on the three dreams. This pursuit ended in a total disaster. I thought the dreams were a sign from God. Talk about misinterpretation! This guy deceived me, hurt me, and left me with a broken heart. A few years later, God showed me that the dreams I had did not mean I was supposed to marry him. Rather, God was showing me the power He had given me to manifest that which I spoke. He wanted me to see that if I spoke something in faith, it could happen. In fact, once I verbalized the dreams, many people who had never heard me speak of it began saying I would marry him. The guy I was dating also had a couple of dreams of marrying me and even went as far as to propose. I declined the proposal because I sought the Lord and knew he was not the one.

Once that saga was over, I began wondering if I had made the wrong decision in not believing my first love. So, I prayed, asked God to help me receive closure and went on with my life. In time, I would date another man who was very romantic and loved to drown me with compliments. Within a few months of dating, he said to me, "God told me you are my wife." I was instantly turned off because I had heard those same words two times before, and both times had ended in shambles. I sought the Lord on his confession, and God said to me that I was only to learn from him. He was not to be the one either.

After that relationship, I realized I kept comparing other men saying, "God said you are my wife," to my first love which assured me, I was not over him. I did not have closure; in fact, I had false closure. But God is so great that He will allow us to come to an awareness about a matter that is unresolved and then grant us the opportunity to receive the closure He knows we desire.

I ran into my first love some years later and had the opportunity to lay out everything—every disappointment, regret and ounce of guilt I had allowed to reside in my heart was finally released. I told him everything. I was even shocked at my own level of transparency, but I knew I had to get it all out if I were going to receive true closure. After I said what needed to be said, I felt a weight lift off my heart. I needed to purge the pain, regret and all of those "what ifs."

As single women who desire true closure, there are some things we must do for ourselves. I had no expectation of what my first love would say or think because my conversation was not about *him*; it was about me receiving the closure I longed for. To that end, I encourage every woman who was or is like me, comparing every man to that one ex you never really got over to do what I did. Maybe you do not have an opportunity to speak to him face to face, but you can write a letter to him and throw it in the ocean, destroy it or have a trusted friend read it out loud.

Spiritually, you can pray and ask God for a divine "divorce." This takes place when the Holy Spirit performs spiritual surgery of your heart; He spiritually divorces you from the lust, desire and/or want for the person from whom you want to be freed. Understand a divine divorce cancels the attachment in the spiritual realm, so it is your responsibility to remain Spirit-led in your decisions. In other words, once God spiritually removes him from your heart, do not get in your flesh and try to reinstate him because doing so will lead to nothing good.

Whatever will help you detach for good, do it! I can testify that I am so free now. I no longer wonder "what-if." When his name is brought up in conversation, I do not feel regret, but I say or think "light and love,"[3] which is a saying I picked up from the movie *Eat Pray Love*. For me, it simply means I wish him light to see God's plan for his life and the love of God to be His portion.

You can do the same. It really works! I pray you find closure in doing these simple but powerful acts. When I was finally able to do this, I knew two things: I was truly single, and I had true closure. My single life was and is no longer complicated but is filled with simplicity as God intends it to be. Yours can be too when you allow your heart to be free from false closures and anything that goes against simplicity.

Confronting Toxic Single Life Perspectives

Whether you view the glass of singleness as half-full or half-empty, you will learn that there are more benefits to be gained from the optimistic approach. A half-empty glass speaks of less opportunity, the end of something or the lack of a thing. However, a glass that is half-full speaks of more opportunity, the continuation of a thing and more of it. For single women, developing a half-full perspective about your life is key.

I am by no means saying single life is a walk in a park. God Himself said, "...It is not good for man to be alone." (Genesis 2:18) However, your perspective can make it seem all bad when in reality there is a surplus of good to be gained. Too often single women develop toxic single-life perspectives such as "I will never find the one," "they are all the same," or "I am not good enough." Such negative perspectives work to complicate a person's single life. Rather than focusing on the opportunities single life presents, women fall into the trap of resenting being single. This mindset is often due to a lack of proper perspective on their single life. Newsflash! Being single has an enormous amount of benefits attached to it.

As I shared at the opening of this book, I am single by choice and genuinely content. I have come to realize that if you allow your singleness to gift you, it will. Some people refer to singleness as a "gift and a curse" but I believe singleness is what you make it. Personally, I have made it a gift-giver which allows me to benefit from it. I view it as a valuable opportunity that could gift us when we develop the proper viewpoint.

I want to share a few of the gifts I have received from singleness in hopes to help you rid yourself of toxic single life perspectives.

5 Gifts of Singleness

The Gift of Aloneness

One toxic single life perspective I would like to dismantle is the idea that being alone equates to being miserable. Let us begin the dismantling, shall we? I remember the first time I ate alone like It was yesterday. It was after the breakup I noted earlier in this chapter. I had become so invested in the wrong person that it almost felt like something was missing if he were not with me. We loved going out to restaurants for dinner and did so quite often. It became second nature that if I were eating, he would be too and vice versa. However, I realized that the missing key to mending my broken heart was found in my ability to create a new normal. So, I started by closing all doors of communication. Once communication ceased, my next step was to normalize his non-existence. In other words, I needed to make that which was abnormal (being without him) normal in my life. I did so by taking a bold step and eating dinner alone at a nice restaurant. At first, my table for one was a little strange as people were staring at me for reasons unknown however I pressed on and tried new restaurants. In time, me, myself and I embraced and even enjoyed eating alone. It became such a great learning experience. I no longer had to entertain unwanted conversation, offer forced responses or show fake interest in topics I could care less about. In essence, I could be me with me and learn a whole lot about me all at once. Being alone gave me the opportunity to hear and consider my own thoughts. It also allowed me to eat as much as I wanted and to be as messy as I wanted while eating.

A significant part of developing a positive perspective on my singleness was spending time with me. My dear sister, make time for you. A great deal of women do not enjoy their single lives because they fill what should be alone time with a new man, a career or a hobby that distracts them from the fact that they need to take time to better their perspective. The gift of aloneness has the power to heal negative perspectives that cannot be gained in the presence of other people. To gain inner healing, you need time for your heart to beat in a new space. Aloneness allows you to create new patterns and teach yourself new lessons in a new space.

Eating alone may seem like small victory to some, but each one builds on another. The building of small victories results in greater ones, which was my finding contentment in being alone. The truth is, I began to enjoy being alone so much I would purposely decline invitations so I could take myself out to dinner. I became comfortable by myself and did not fear that I would look like a loser because I did not have anyone sitting across from me. Being alone became liberating. It can be compared to that feeling we get when we cut, color, or change our hair after a breakup. I am sure you know the feeling, if not, ask a sister friend – I am sure she will know.

Question, are you okay being alone? If not, take time on your journey to figure out why that is, then strive to correct your perspective. There may be deep truths pertaining to self-awareness that you should consider while you are unmarried. I strongly believe in faith-based and professional mental health counseling. I want to break the stigma that sometimes is present in church or different ethnic communities – therapy is not for "crazy" people. Instead, like any other part of your body—your mind can require treatment that will cause it to work better.

I encourage every single woman who struggles with alone time or anything of that nature to consult a professional. Chances are you need to take time to work on your emotional self. The more you give your emotions the chance to be processed, the better equipped you will be to emotionally engage in future relationships. After the toxic relationship I mentioned earlier in this chapter, I sought a licensed counselor who helped me to process the hurt I experienced. It was my first time in a therapy session, and I must say, it exceeded my expectation. I am normally the sister whom everyone else comes to vent to, for advice or problem solve so being able to share with someone else was extremely freeing. I am wholeheartedly a proponent of Jesus and therapy. I believe the Lord equips human beings with expertise to care for our natural needs. After spending time with Jesus and a therapist, you will come to realize God has uniquely made you great, so who better to be alone with than you?

As uncomfortable as it may be in the initial stages, I encourage every reader to enter a season of aloneness. When we are routinely in relationships, friendships or in the company of other people, it is impossible to unwrap the gift of aloneness. During my time alone, in addition to the first gift noted, I also discovered four additional gifts. All five gifts are available to anyone willing to shift their perspective.

Biblically speaking, five is the number of grace or God's free gift to us nondependent on any merit of our own. When we develop the proper perspective, we will more easily see that God has given us the grace to change our outlook for the better. Now, for the next four gifts: hurt, healing, wholeness and security.

The Gift of Hurt

Another toxic single life perspective is the idea that single women are damaged goods. This concept is usually linked to unprocessed hurt from past relationships. As ridiculous as this may sound, when I altered my point of view, I found hurt to be a gift. What brought me to this conclusion was gaining the awareness of owning my part in my own hurt. It is easier to identify a scapegoat when it is anyone other than you. However, I came to realize that unless I owned my individual part in being hurt, I would never be fully healed. When we focus solely on the part the opponent (i.e. an ex) played – we remain victims to the shackles of hurt. We must own the fact that we stayed too long or gave too many chances or ignored the red flags. By taking responsibility, it allows us to change the way we view hurt. Let me explain, without hurt, we would never appreciate healing. Hurt teaches us a lesson that happiness cannot, which is you can survive the pain. This truth will help you when you decide to entertain a new relationship. Even if pain is or becomes a part of that relationship, you know you will survive after it. Psalms 30:5b states, "...*weeping may endure for a night, but joy cometh in the morning.*"

Being alone showed me how hurt I really was by my past and present realities. That deep hurt led to tears that needed to be shed. There are tears that must fall in order to let the sting of hurt go. Yes, weeping is necessary. Holding in difficult emotions and expecting to be healed is unhealthy and unrealistic. Rather, releasing the sadness, anger, disappointment, hurt, etc., enables us to move forward from it. You cannot overcome what you will not confront. Be courageous and face the hurt. Personally, confronting my hurt forced me to own my part in the matter which led to a necessary forgiving of myself.

I urge each woman who has been hurt to own the part you played and forgive yourself. Perhaps, you were just upset at yourself for allowing "it" to happen. If so, forgive you and let it go. It was meant to teach you a lesson...have you learned that lesson? If not, chances are you will keep being hurt in the same or similar ways until you learn the lesson the gift of hurt wishes to teach you. When you allow yourself to be open to the lesson, you will no longer be susceptible to the same cycle of hurt.

Instead, you will recognize it before it has the chance to impact you in your future.

The Gift of Healing

The next toxic single life perspective is the notion that single women are too bitter to embrace healing. This idea is typically the result of statements or actions single women use to express dissatisfaction with the opposite sex. What commonly lies underneath those statements or actions are our choices to prematurely enter relationships without taking the proper time to heal after heartbreak. Therefore, what may come across as anger likely is unprocessed feelings of resentment, betrayal etc. No wonder so many "rebound relationships" do not work. Attempting to bounce a deflated basketball off the backboard and into the net is useless because the ball has no air. This illustration is why women end up with so many back-to-back breakups because they attempted to fill their deflated hearts with a man rather than address the pain that caused the deflation in the first place.

Heartbreak cannot be healed with a simple bandage; on the contrary, heartbreak can range from minor to major surgery. As a chaplain, I have met innumerable persons who upon losing their spouse end up in the hospital with some sort of heart complication. Some even die of what is deemed as "dying of a broken heart." The heart is an extraordinarily strong yet sensitive organ that produces blood naturally and love emotionally. When that love experiences a loss due to death, divorce or breakup, enormous pain is felt deeply. If the proper healing is not attained, the heart will eventually stop—emotionally and/or physically. Not being healed emotionally of a broken heart can prevent a person from loving again. Physically, it can literally lead to a heart attack or death. Therefore, we should embrace the gift of healing. So how do you heal a broken heart? Psychology suggests, "If you're looking to boost your happiness, try faking it. Called *the facial feedback hypothesis*, engaging in the physical, muscular act of smiling can send signals to your brain that you *are* happy."[4]

I happen to disagree with this theory because sending a false sense of happiness to a shattered broken heart may change the person's mood momentarily, but it will not fix it permanently. Those who desire healing want it to be permanent rather than a quick fix. The Bible teaches us that God Himself "heals the brokenhearted and binds up their wounds." (Ps 147:3) The Hebrew word for healing in this verse is *raphe*, which translates as "to sew together or to mend."[5] This means God literally takes the shattered pieces of our hearts and mends them together.

Oftentimes when we try to self-medicate, we end up having a half-hearted fix rather than a wholehearted one. This is because we did not create our hearts; God did. Therefore, we must give our broken hearts back to the Divine Manufacturer. Aren't you sick of quick fixes? It is your time to receive permanent healing by giving your heart to the permanent Healer.

The Gift of Wholeness

The next toxic perspective is the thought that single women cannot be whole without a man. Before I was licensed and ordained, my very first sermon I ever preached to family and friends was entitled "The Heart of the Church." God told me to draw half of a heart and turn it in different directions while asking those gathered what it was. Well, no one guessed accurately. Then He led me to make this point: "When you do anything half-heartedly, it can be misinterpreted." Let us stop at this point for a second. If you are in a relationship at the present, are you in it half-heartedly? What about your single life? Are you in it half-heartedly? Let us take it a step further. Have you been guilty of having a half-hearted relationship with God? Many women are in half-hearted relationships with God and wonder why the right man is not finding them. The only way to be in a wholehearted relationship with God is to do what the word implies—give God your *whole* heart!

To break free from this perspective, we must be sure that we do not possess any of its characteristics. A sure sign that you are not whole in your singleness is what you will allow or entertain from a man. Women who are not whole in their singleness settle by accepting less than what they deserve from men. Oftentimes a woman tolerates forms of neglect or abuse because he is her imaginary ticket out of singleness. In essence, women accept less because they want to feel as if they are not totally single. By accepting "no title," "just friends," or things of that nature, women who are looking for commitment will unfortunately find disappointment. By not requiring more from him in the first place, you have set the tone of your relationship. When you let him reap the benefits of commitment without one, you more than likely will never get one. You will end up regretting the time you wasted, hoping things would change. So, if you fall into the "he-just-will-not-commit" category, the time has come to evaluate what standard you have set. If it cannot be changed, let it go. Accept it for what it was—a poor decision made from an emotionally distorted place because you were not whole.

However, the way to become whole and not fall subject to this mentality is to become clear. Be clear on your own intentions, your goals, your desires and above all your standards. When you rid yourself of uncertainty and become direct and unwavering you will leave no room for misinterpretation or miscommunication. When you have clarity as to what it is you want, you will not waste time settling for relationships that do not offer it. When a woman is whole, she can set clear standards for herself as to what she wants in a relationship and what she absolutely will not settle for. Such standards will allow you to quickly rid your space of those who do not fit the standard and make room for those who do.

So how do you attain wholeness in singleness? Glad you asked. I believe it is attained by taking time to work on the emotional, physical, financial, intellectual, and spiritual you. Although that sounds like a mouthful, it is not impossible as I intentionally took time off from dating to work on all five above stated areas. It is not a walk in the park, but it is extremely beneficial. For emotional wellness, I began working with a professional counselor. For my physical well-being, I started working out four times a week. Financially, I researched how the stock market worked and began investing my money more wisely. Intellectually, I enrolled in a doctoral program which I finally took off my bucket list.

Finally, spiritually I developed a more intentional and targeted prayer life. As single women, one of the best ways to build a healthy perspective is to maximize the time we have to work on us. I believe the difference between a whole woman and a broken woman is the way in which they use their time. A whole woman knows how to use her time wisely while the broken woman knows how to waste her time foolishly. Choose which one you will be wisely. The decision you make today can impact the future you.

Now, embracing the gift of wholeness allows you to develop the ability to speak a language I like to call "whole singleness." This language does not contain sad words, hopeless statements, or dreary proclamations about your single life. It embraces the benefits of single life and is filled with positive affirmations about present realities. You begin unwrapping the gift of wholeness when you rid your dialogue of those habitual ways of speaking about your single life. Along with seeking God, taking time to heal, and setting standards, you can also speak yourself into wholeness. Proverbs 18:21, *"Death and life are in the power of the tongue: and they that love it shall eat the fruit thereof."* If you begin to speak in faith daily that you are whole in your mind, body, soul and heart, you will become that which you speak. *Speaking in faith* means "I believe it before I see it." Even if you feel sad one day about being single, speak in faith that you have the joy of the Lord in your singleness. When you believe what you say aloud, it has the power to counteract what you feel. Read that again. Feelings are not more powerful than faith. Therefore, feelings should never overrule faith. Hence why you must speak in faith at the onset of negative feelings.

In my first book, *Birthing Purpose Against All Odds*, I included an in-depth section on the power of verbal declarations. I received several compelling testimonies from those who took action. Therefore, I admonish every woman who reads this book and struggles with speaking negatively about their single life to begin declaring God's word over her single life. The following are some scriptures to get you started:

"And ye are complete in him, which is the head of all principality and power." (Colossians 2:10)

"Delight thyself also in the LORD; and he shall give thee the desires of thine heart." (Psalm 37:4)

You may be wondering: Is this really all I need to do to be whole? Of course not. However, if I encouraged you, the reader, to work out (be physically whole), speak to your pastor (be spiritually whole), speak to a counselor (be emotionally whole) and you continued to speak negatively, all of these three efforts would be in vain. Therefore, do not simply *begin* acting but *continue* the action taken. Remember, wholeness is a lifelong continued work as we are ever evolving.

The Gift of Security

The last toxic single life perspective I would like to address is the idea that single women are insecure. This concept comes from the belief that single women look for men to make them feel secure. Now, we are familiar with the "good girls like bad boys" philosophy which I believe is true because bad boys somehow offer good girls a sense of security. I want to take that proposal a step further. Not only good girls but also good women can fall for bad men in hopes to find security. However, if a woman desires to feel safe or secure with a man, it does not imply that she is insecure. To the contrary, as it is quite common for a woman who *is* secure to seek a man who is also secure. Secure women are generally not attracted to insecure men, as they see their insecurity as a turn off.

On the other hand, we will consider the possibility that some single women do seek security in a man. Physical or emotional security may be found in the toughest of men however if that man becomes ill or permanently disabled where does a woman's security lie? When we trust in arms of flesh, we set ourselves up to endless limitations and inevitable disappointment. Truth of the matter is, God is the only One who can see, know, and understand when danger will be apparent. This means He alone is our supreme source of security. Man's limited ability to protect a woman does not hold a candle to the omnipresent, limitless security of God. Be sure to embrace the gift of security as it presents single women with the opportunity to find true protection in the Lord.

Psalm 46:1 says it this way, *"God is our refuge and strength, a very present help in trouble."* The word for *refuge* in its original Hebrew form is *machaceh*[6], which means shelter from storm, rain or danger. Emotional, physical, financial, and social storms will come into a single woman's life at the most inopportune times. Without the security of the Lord, these storms can overwhelm us. Single sisters, you may sometimes feel like the rain in those torrential storms will drown you, but when your security is rooted in the Lord, you can rest assured in His stability. No matter how stormy your single life will be, you will weather the storm.

II - *Sexy*

The Rings

When I was in high school, I was quite popular mainly

because I was a part of the "in crowd" and a confident all-league, all-county, all-state track star. As I got older, the popularity, praise and admiration caused me to develop this idea that everything about me had to be sexy. I trained intensely until I had the "perfect body," which led to even more popularity. Then, I dyed half of my hair honey-blonde and the other half jet-black. I also wore hazel contacts just to avoid wearing prescription glasses that would "kill" my image. Not to mention, I dressed fashionably, never missed a mani/pedi day and dated the cutest, most popular boys in school.

My socially-imposed need to be sexy led me to secretly go to Jamaica Avenue in Queens, New York, to get my belly button pierced without my parents' awareness or approval. Although, I never got into trouble with the law, it is safe to say that I had a common case of the "Teenage-I-Do-What-I-Want-Its" Attitude. As long as what I did was not hurting anyone, I did it. I knew my parents would be disappointed and even angry about the belly piercing, so I hid what I had done from them. I would have caused my mother great worry had she known of the re-piercings I had to undergo because the belly ring kept falling out causing the previously pierced hole to close. Thanks to my super-flat, six-pack, track-star stomach, the bar that was used to hold the ring in place did not have enough skin to remain attached. The bar fell out three times, creating the need to be pierced again. When all was said and done, I ended up with a top and a bottom belly button ring. Once these were finally in place, no one could tell me anything. I felt so sexy and was constantly told how sexy I was—especially when I would flaunt my shiny, pink and gold dangling belly rings.

In my mind, I was Beyoncé, and my friends were members of Destiny's Child. A number of my classmates began copying my style and became fluent in "Daph-ology," the term one of my classmates coined to describe the various phrases I used in daily conversation that spread through the high school like wildfire. Many mimicked my personality, fashion sense and slang. It felt as though I was a local celebrity for sure. Feeling sexy made me think I was an adult. So, the sexier I felt, the more adult activities I embraced. These escapades that started in high school lasted for about a year and a half into my undergraduate college career at Dowling College in Oakdale, NY where I studied to become a secondary education English teacher.

I remember the time after my sophomore year in college that my entire life changed forever like it was yesterday. On a cold autumn day, one of my classmates invited me to a Christian youth program that our college youth ministry was hosting on campus. I decided to attend, and there I met a minister who spoke about the "Joshua generation." She preached with such passion that I felt convicted in my spirit about all the wrong activities I was embracing. I felt that God wanted more from me and that the sinful life I was living was not pleasing to Him.

As I walked back to my dorm room at the conclusion of the program, I began weeping. When I went inside, I told my roommate about my experience and only began to weep even more. I knew God wanted something from me, but I did not know what. I prayed that night and felt that God wanted me to end the relationship in which I was involved at the time. It was with my "first love." We were together for five years; he had set me on a pedestal and practically kissed the ground I walked on. I was deeply saddened that God would want me to end it.

The next day I mustered up the courage to do what God wanted me to do and break up with him. Within a few months, I was soon involved in another relationship with a "bad boy" who I later discovered was a drug dealer. Little did I know I had really hit the furthest thing from the jackpot this time. I found myself torn because I had really grown to like this guy. He would finish my sentences, and seemed to understand me, which is something I had always looked for in a relationship. He made me feel sexy, desirable, and cared for. I thought we had so much in common, not realizing what really drew me to him was the huge void of loneliness I felt after my "first love" and I broke up. Deep down I still felt like God wanted me to do something more and being involved with him would not help me get there. Within six months of contemplating how I would get out of this one, one of my best friends had a car accident that could have been fatal. In some way and somehow, God used my friend's car accident to wake me up from the bed of compromise in which I had become comfortable. I realized how quickly life could be over, and I did not want to live my life outside of God's will anymore, so I ended the relationship.

Nearly four to five months later, a clip of this woman preaching about sexual sin flashed across my television screen, and I could not believe my ears. Growing up in a traditionally Baptist church, I had never heard anyone mention the word *sex*—let alone preach a sermon about it. I wanted to know who this woman was, but I only caught the very end of the clip and was unable to see her name on the screen. About a week or so later I heard her voice again and ran quickly to the television because I had to find out who this woman was. Finally, I caught her name on the screen and wrote it down.

Later that month, my friend and I were in a local shopping store and right in front of me was a DVD with the woman's name I had written down. I gasped in disbelief as I recognized the title of the sermon clip that I had seen on television. I quickly picked up and purchased Dr. Juanita Bynum's DVD "No More Sheets."

During the next week I told all of my friends about this DVD and how I wanted them to watch it with me. As fate would have it, I ended up watching it with only two of my friends who both needed to hear it. The Holy Spirit convicted me and all I could do was cry out to God. By the end of the DVD, the power of God fell so strongly that I ended up in my friend's bed, lying on my back-worshipping God. In that moment, I felt the Spirit of the Lord all over my body, and I heard God say, "Can I trust you to say what I tell you to say? Go where I tell you to go? And do what I tell you to do?"

I said "Yes" to the Lord. Then I felt the Holy Spirit purge my heart, mind, and body from all the indiscretions of old. I repented or felt sorrowful and turned from the bad decisions and deeds of my past and asked Him to forgive me. Not only did He wipe my slate clean, but He delivered me and enabled me to live a pure life before Him. I believed in the supernatural power of God beforehand, but it was not until this very personal experience that I really came to know how powerful God truly was. God had done a supernatural work in me that day, and my life has never been the same.

The night after this unforgettable encounter with God, I felt compelled to remove both of my belly-button rings. God was calling me into something new, and to experience the new, I decided to let go of the old. Removing my two belly rings were much more than appears on the surface. Their removal represented a decision to detach my new self from my old ways and desires. 2 Corinthians 5:17 says, *"If any man be in Christ, he is a new creature, old things are passed away behold all things are become new."* After that supernatural experience, I felt a change within myself. Although I looked the same on the outside, I knew I had been transformed on the inside. I lost the desire go to night clubs, dress provocatively and even fall into temptation with "bad boys."

Being free from that which went against Christ allowed me to be in a right relationship with Him. I had been thinking and living in error, so once Christ cleaned up my life, I did not want anything to identify me with my old ways. These choices were the result of my own personal conviction; in no way am I saying that someone with a piercing cannot be in Christ. Christ is concerned about our hearts—not our outward appearance. However, for me in that moment, I knew God wanted me to be free from the need to be "sexy" because I then equated it with sin. So, after experiencing my inner transformation, I made an outward proclamation.

In time, as Christ began to transform my mind, I came to discover **being sexy is not sinful when it is done the right way.** We will further explore this concept later in this chapter. Celebrities dress provocatively, sing, dance, act, or speak in ways that equate being sexy with being promiscuous. However, sexy does not have to lead to any type of sinful behavior. With that being stated, I agree with Merriam Webster's definition of *sexy* which is "1) sexually suggestive or stimulating; 2) attractive or appealing."[7] When the first meaning is considered within the bonds of matrimony, the usage is not sinful. The second meaning can be used to describe one who carries herself with an assured confidence. Therefore, sexiness has nothing to do with what a woman wears, what she has pierced, or how she wears her hair or makeup. Sexiness goes much deeper than that. It is wrapped up in a woman's level of confidence and how she shows up in a room.

She & He

As a woman, you have the power to command attention anywhere you go simply by owning your sexy by walking in confidence. Society pressures us as women every day to look and/or dress a certain way to be considered desirable. For centuries we have been subjected to statements like, "IF you lost some weight...", "IF you didn't show your shape...", "IF you weren't so skinny..." THEN you would be more appealing to whomever. These statements are dangerous to one's psyche because they have the power to create a mentality of insufficiency. It gives the sense that one is not enough currently and must do something to become enough. Such words promote a sense of worthlessness by which one must try to become worthy in the sight of another. This sort of commentary leaves no room for the listener to decide whether or not they themselves are content with how they appear. In essence, a woman could potentially have been pleased with what she saw in the mirror however after hearing one or more "if/then" remarks, she could be left questioning. These sorts of statements have led women to question themselves and, in some cases, alter who they are to appease other people. Many have starved themselves, overeaten and even gone under the knife for enlargements or reductions to their bodies. Simply put, **many have become someone they were not to please people who did not value who they truly were.**

It is crucial that we, as women are content with who we see in the mirror. It is vital that we appreciate, embrace, and celebrate that woman who stares back at us in our reflection. Recognizing, she has sustained struggles that others have not lived to talk about. She gives birth to creation and it becomes doctors, lawyers, presidents, inventors etc. She adopts, fosters, mothers' children she did not birth as her very own because it is who she is. She was created by God because it was not good for man to be alone. Man, as strong, macho, and mighty as he can be — needed a helper, a nurturer, a woman to be as effective and efficient as he could be as a man. I once heard a preacher suggest that God created man then had a better idea, so He made woman. Of course, he was being facetious however it does shed light on a woman's ability to bring out the absolute best in a man. Every Martin needs a Coretta just as every Barack needs a Michelle. Women are powerful. Women receive a seed and bring forth a baby. Women have only a can of beans and produce full meals that may last a week. Historically, women have been held back in society but have broken glass ceilings and campaigned for the highest office in the land. What am I saying? Glad you asked. Women were created with the God-given ability to enhance whatever is given to them — including her natural beauty. Therefore, it is imperative that we are resolute in the fact that the God within us has created us to be beautiful, brilliant, and yes, even sexy. I do not know who needs to hear this but: it is wonderful to be saved and sexy! You do not need to dress like a mummy to prove you love Jesus.

We were created in the image and likeness of God, Himself. This means we resemble the immaculate, pure, and holy God. Is there anyone more beautiful? Absolutely not! He is the epitome of beauty not to mention the actual Creator of it. Therefore, real beauty is only found in Him. When we, too are found in Him then real beauty is also found in us. Regardless as to how much money is spent or silicone is used, true beauty is not found outside of Him. Anything that man creates and deems "beautiful" was made by creation whom God Himself created. Therefore, any creativity that comes out of creation was *first* derived out of God. He placed His creative power inside of us, enabling us to create. The most skilled painter can create a well-detailed and exquisite painting of the sky, but it does not compare to the magnificent beauty revealed by the actual, divinely designed sky. The same God who created the adored Moon, the mysterious Sun, the glistening stars also took time to strategically create you. Nothing man can manufacture will ever be more beautiful than what God creates. Since God created you, nothing is more beautiful than you.

Owning the beauty of who you are internally is key in establishing your sense of sexy externally. Without this key, people will project on to you what sexy should be for you. I want to challenge each woman to embrace sexy on your own terms. Resist the need to fit in any box this world has created for you. Dare to dress, style, think, walk, talk and most importantly live outside of the box. Forget what your mother, aunt or best friend told or showed you sexy was. Make the decision to define it for yourself. This will free you from the draining need to honor the opinions of others while downplaying your own.

The Queen

As promised earlier in this chapter, let us delve deeper into the concept of sexy is not sinful when it is done the right way. For starters, the Bible tells the story of a beautiful, attractive woman by the name of Esther who, in twenty-first century lingo, would be considered sexy. She had the power to command attention in a room. In fact, her beauty granted her so much special attention that she won the favor of a man named Hegai, who was responsible for preparing the women to meet the king. She was so appealing and confident that she stood out from all the other women who had gathered in hopes to become the next queen to wed King Ahasuerus. Without engaging in sinful sexual acts, Esther was sexy personified.

It is interesting to note that the book of Esther never uses the name "God." However, Scripture reveals that promotion comes from the Lord (Psalm 75:6). Therefore, my belief is that Esther was chosen for such a lofty position as a result of God's divine favor. All the other sexy women were dolled up in hopes to win the beauty pageant, but only one was crowned queen. Here is the key: **sexiness will get you in a contest (commonplace), but favor will give you the throne (uncommon place)**.

My dear sisters, you are queens and should recognize yourself as such. I do not believe we were created to aspire to the commonplace; I believe we were created to thrive in the uncommon place. After all, Scripture reveals that we are a royal priesthood (1 Peter 2:9) and heirs of God (Romans 8:17) or citizens of the kingdom of Heaven. In essence, if you are a child of God, you are royalty!

Royalty means you have a right to the uncommon place! The uncommon place is the place where you are treated with the utmost respect and dignity simply because you are a queen. So, what is stopping you from getting there? Do you have the wrong understanding of sexy? Or have you settled for common so much in your past that you do not realize you deserve better in your future? Take a moment to think about those two questions and continue reading after you have arrived at you answer.

More Than Sexy

There is a clear distinction between a sexy woman and a favored woman. A sexy woman is confident in herself (looks, talents, success, etc.) alone. A favored woman is confident in the God who gave her the looks, talents, success, etc. There are limitations to what a sexy woman can receive while the favored woman has no limitations. Instead, she recognizes that the only reason she is beautiful is because God has made her in His image and in His likeness. The humility she exhibits is what attracts the favor of God upon her life. James 4:6 states, "...*God resists the proud, but gives grace to the humble.*" The word used for *grace* in the original Greek form also means "favor." [8] Therefore, the more humble one is the more favor the Lord will release over her life. When a woman is humbly sexy, there is no limit to what God will do in her life.

Perhaps the reason so many women are only sexy and not favored lies in the fact that they are too proud. Being proud or prideful is often used as a cover up to conceal something much deeper. Pride is a common mask of choice worn to cover hurt, rejection, abuse, neglect, fear or pain of many sorts. However, if a woman desires to be favored, she must detach herself from pride, which prevents God's favor.

Perhaps the reason why so many women remain in dysfunctional relationships is because pride will not let them walk away. Pride keeps women entangled in miserable relationships for the sake of maintaining an image before people who do not even matter. Yes, I said it because it is true. Half of the people you may be trying to "keep face" in front of do not even speak to you on a daily basis; they are your social media friends only or they, too, are hiding behind masks. What do you get out of suffering in a broken friendship, relationship, or marriage? The sad reality is many women allow pride to trick them into keeping something alive that had already died. A broken heart, a confused mind and a resentful spirit are the result of holding on to a dead relationship. These choices keep you in the commonplace.

In order to go beyond the commonplace, you must identify what is keeping you there. Although there are many contributing factors, we will discuss the following: the past, addressing the pain, overcoming emotional triggers and forgiveness.

Past

Without a realistic evaluation of one's past, thinking one's present will magically lead to a beautiful future is easy. When a woman is not over her past, she will keep finding men to distract her from the reality of her unprocessed emotions of old. Single sisters, the same wound can only be wounded again when it is still opened. If you constantly find the same kind of men or attract the same kind of men , chances are you have not taken time to free your mind, body and spirit from the man who wounded you. Until you do, you will not have room in your heart for the right one—even if you meet him. It is possible to meet the right man and it still not work out because you have no space in your heart for him.

Your past can hold you hostage for the rest of your life if you allow it to do so. To obtain what you deserve, you must be freed from the pain of your past. This, my dear sister, is a trick of the commonplace. There is comfortability in going with what you know simply because you know what to expect. However, knowing what you expect and knowing what you deserve are two different matters. You can expect the common without realizing you deserve the uncommon. The uncommon is the road less traveled because it is uncomfortable. Addressing past pains that have broken your heart, left you with emotional triggers and understandable unforgiveness is uncomfortable. It is not easy. Although not easy, confronting them is not impossible!

Addressing the Pain

Another factor that keeps us in the common place is our failure to address our pain. By nature, women go through a lifetime of difficult or painful events (menstruation, childbirth and even menopause, to name only a few). As we age from childhood to adulthood, some of us get married or divorced, have children, adopt children or are ill-equipped to parent and choose to give them away. We advance in our careers, but even in a millennial age still experience earning gaps. In 2011, studies revealed that women who worked full-time jobs earned 82.8% of what their male coworkers earned.[9] Among some sects of Christian Evangelicals, Roman Catholics and Jewish believers alike, discrimination against women still exists.

These disparities do not begin to reflect the following deplorable statistics that illustrate the unimaginable pain to which women are subjected. Take a deep breath as these next few sentences are heavy hearted. In the United States of America, 1 in 5 women have been raped and every nine seconds.[10] These numbers do not include the millions of women who do not report being raped or assaulted. I am including these statistics to bring a greater awareness of the severity of the pain women suffer in silence. Many women are too embarrassed, hurt or afraid to share of their experience/s of sexual, verbal or physical abuse. When we are unable to share, we often do not seek proper help in addressing our pains. As an unfortunate result, we continue to develop and repeat dangerous cycles and even normalize them.

It is no secret that the first step to getting help is to admit that one has a problem. Whether mental, emotional, physical, social or spiritual, all problems are capable of being solved. The pain does not have to keep you from what God intends for you to have which is healing. God did not create us to dwell in a place of pain; rather, He created us to thrive in a place of healing. Once silent pain is addressed, it no longer has the power to keep us trapped in fear or anger. Many women who are labeled as "angry, mean-spirited or bitter" are often women who have never addressed their pasts pain.

To take it a step further, as a Shinnecock Native-American and African American woman, historically both sides of my culture were reared not to talk about painful or even traumatic events that have happened. As I grew older and gained friends of various races, I learned that my culture was not alone in their silent pain. Many other cultures such as the Irish and Asian to name a couple, also are taught not to confront the pains of the past. Therefore, not addressing pain goes deeper than a cultural issue; it is a human issue. By using a defense mechanism, whether it be avoidance or denial, women and men alike have been inadvertently trained not to voice their painful emotions. As single women, this is one of the most common yet unhealthy practices to date. The more a person fails to address his or her painful experiences, the more their suppressed pains will come to light in their interpersonal relationships. As a professional healthcare chaplain, I have encountered many female patients who have admitted to becoming intimate with other women because of the scars men have left on their hearts. However, many fail to overcome the hurt and repeat the same unhealthy patterns with woman as they did with men. This is also true of heterosexual women who have been hurt by careless men and repeatedly seek the same type of men. These patterns are rooted in unaddressed pain coupled with unprocessed emotions.

It is equally important to note, if a young boy grows up watching his father physically abuse his mother, he has a higher probability of growing up and repeating this reprehensible behavior. Studies show "Children of domestic violence are 3 times more likely to repeat the cycle in adulthood."[11] This unfortunate reality is the result of individuals failing to seek any professional help, spiritual guidance or emotional support after experiencing trauma. This factual finding can be used to understand many factors in dysfunctional relationships and help to answer why women habitually find themselves entertaining the same unhealthy behaviors from men. The only way for women to break this habit is by taking action. No one will force you to be healed of the hurts you have suffered. You must want your healing more than you want your hurt. Although you may have normalized your hurt, you deserve better! You deserve to smile and laugh from a genuine place. You must realize you deserve more than what your hurt has to offer you. When you find yourself more drawn to healing than hurt is when you know you have found the strength to address the pain. You deserve to have joy within you that you cannot articulate. The joy of a woman who addresses her pain without remaining a slave to it is unexplainable. It can only be experienced. Are you ready to experience it? I certainly hope so and want to help you do so. I have included a short yet powerful 3-step guide at the end of this section to help you get started.

God allowed me to identify an unhealthy cycle in my own life concerning my breaking up with good guys for seemingly no reason. I had unwittingly developed a defense mechanism of detaching from them before they had an opportunity to hurt me. This escape mechanism was the result of my not taking time to address my internal pain. Once I understood the issue, I began to pray and ask God to heal my heart. Within a few months, I found myself in a Clinical Pastoral Education program (required for professional Chaplaincy) where I had to confront the painful heartaches I experienced. Although I was nervous, I discovered owning and naming my pain felt like a weight had been taken off my chest; I felt unshackled. Therefore, I encourage you to read and apply this short 3-step guide to begin your healing journey.

I. *Choose a specific time to pray (preferably morning) and stick to it.*

Prayer creates a line of communication with the One who created you. Above all else, you need to talk with God daily as He knows exactly how to heal, mend, and restore you. Consistency is key so by selecting a specific time, your heart and mind will become accustomed to setting a daily intention. When you set your intention in prayer, it will direct your day. The key to prayer is believing what you are praying has already happened. In other words, faith is the key therefore pray in faith always. Earnestly open your heart and mind and be upfront with God. Do not hold back anything. He knows everything, anyway. So, be totally transparent with Him as you share what and who has hurt you. Ask Him to heal your pain and be specific. Whether it is mental, emotional, physical etc., tell Him all about it. Ask Him to give you the strength to address, process and forgive each area that is impacting your life. Then, ask Him to help you establish a healthy outlook. Continue prayer daily for as long as it takes until the pain becomes a thing of the past.

II.   *Find Scriptures that speak to your pain, meditate on them, and apply them in your life.*

The word of God is the most powerful tool we have as believers to confront any adversary whether natural or supernatural. Your healing process includes both as you desire your natural heart to stop hurting and your spiritual heart to be made whole. Meditating on Gods word is quite effective at overcoming negative thoughts in your mind and behaviors in your life. For first timers, you meditate by selecting a scripture that best speaks to your pain. If you are not sure where to start, I will include a few freebees at the end of this section. Once you select a Scripture, write it down and say it aloud (approx. 7 times) to help you commit it to memory. Feel free to play relaxing music that will allow you to be still and absorb God's word into your spirit. Continue this until you no longer need the paper as a reference. Post the Scripture on a wall, desk, door close to you so it is the first thing you see in the morning. Then, find a way daily to apply the Scripture in your life. For instance, if you meditate on Proverbs 18:24 which refers to showing yourself friendly, then practice ways of doing so. Perhaps, smiling more or intentionally being kind to a stranger. The more you apply the Word of God, the more it will transform you. This means the more time you take to meditate on healing Scriptures, the more your hurt will cease.

As a bonus, meditation affords God the opportunity to renew your mind. He simply needs you to agree with its being renewed. Oftentimes our mindset keeps us in a place of hurt which is why it must be renewed. For instance, I allowed my past hurts to motivate me to push good guys away because of the hurt I had experienced when I had allowed others into my life. I thought it was best to push them away to avoid getting hurt. However, this negative mindset is not how God would have me to think. This was my own understanding and one not rooted in God's Word.

Single sisters, how many times have you made a relational decision based on your own understanding instead of God's Word? One Scripture that helped me in this area was Proverbs 3:5 and 6, which says, *"Trust in the LORD with all thine heart and lean not unto thine own understanding. In all thy ways acknowledge Him, and he shall direct thy paths."* Our understanding is inferior to God's which is why we should meditate on His word and allow Him to renew our minds. Our understanding can lead to fear, paranoia, and confusion—none of which are of God. Since He is all knowing, it is impossible for our finite minds to ever possess the amount of understanding that His mind has. Because of this impossibility, we must allow God to renew our minds. As promised earlier, here are those freebee Scriptures that will help you get started on your healing journey: *Isaiah 53:4, 5; 2 Corinthians 5:17 and Psalm 47:3.*

III.   *Consult Professional Help*

Along with the spiritual resources, natural resources can be highly effective at supporting you in addressing your pain and receiving complete healing. Speak with a professional mental health counselor, a spiritual advisor, a professional chaplain, or someone who is trained to help you process your mental, spiritual, and emotional pains. In the section entitled "Gift of Aloneness," in chapter one, I took the time to celebrate how vitally important counseling is on your single life journey. Feel free to refer back to it. Without being repetitive, I will simply say to those who may be skeptical about seeking professional help, you deserve to give yourself every single opportunity to heal. Counseling is yet another opportunity that can help you in ways you may not realize you need. Be sure to check reviews and secure a counselor who has both the skill and heart for helping others.

Overcoming Emotional Triggers

When I broke up with my first love, I could not listen to a certain singer on the radio because hearing his voice would instantly bring tears to my eyes. I remembered how much we loved this singer, how we would often play his CD and so many other positive memories attached to his songs. Emotional triggers can be likened to red flags that go off in your heart, mind and body to alert you of something that has happened in the past that you are connecting to a present situation. When a trigger is pushed, you may respond very negatively in anger, fear, rage or even sadness. On your single life journey, it is important to be aware of your emotional triggers and develop ways to cope with them while you are going through your healing process.

One of the common practices in trauma therapy is to have a client repeat the details of a traumatic incident aloud. Repetition allows the person to hear himself or herself aloud while experiencing all the feelings tied to the event. This helps the individual to process the difficult emotions that are often ignored or left unaddressed.

This same practice can also be used to overcome an emotional trigger which is the next factor that contributes to our remaining in the common place. By taking time to tell someone what happened or say aloud to yourself what triggers you emotionally (for example, someone calls you overweight as an adult) and why it triggers you (your parents called you overweight as a child) will help to take the initial sting out of your emotional trigger. The power of that trigger lessens as you repeat your story, which allows you to own what has happened and no longer allow it to own you. Whatever happened to you does not have the power to define you unless you allow it to do so. Emotional triggers are often mistakenly equated to "personality." However, your personality is who you were before the emotional trigger became a part of you.

An emotional trigger is not your personality; it is your response to a bad event or memory which may have changed your personality (usually in an unfavorable way). Nevertheless, practicing repetition and owning what has happened will help you to make meaning of the incident. Once you find meaning such as "I was young and can no longer blame myself for not knowing what I did not know," or "My heartbreak was necessary because without it, I would have never known what true love (the love of God) felt like," or "If people never said I would not succeed, I would have never realized how much success God had in store for me." Once you establish meaning to what previously pained you, you can **forgive**. Yes, forgiveness is a major part of overcoming an emotional trigger.

Most emotional triggers are the direct result of what someone has done to us. So, when we forgive, we will no longer be held captive by the trigger that person left us with when we were hurt. Forgiveness gives us back the power someone took from us. For example, you did not have a trust issue until you were lied to. You were not afraid of the dark until you were attacked in the dark. You were not afraid of small spaces until you were locked in a small space. If you want to be free, FORGIVE those who hurt you! Hasn't this trigger taken up enough space in your mind and heart? The time has come for you to be free!

Forgiveness

Jesus told the disciples that before prayer, they must forgive anyone against whom they had ought so that God may forgive them. This command is not only restricted to prayer but is necessary for daily life. The greatest gift of forgiveness is that you too are forgiven by God. On the contrary, your being unforgiving prevents you from receiving God's forgiveness. Check out Matthew 6:15, where Jesus makes clear to commune or connect with Him with Him, one must have a clear pathway. This means nothing should stand in the way of one's communication or relationship with Christ. Unforgiveness gets in the way of your relationship with God because it goes deep into your heart—the very place from which your belief in God emanates. Remember, we receive salvation when we confess with our mouths and believe in our **hearts** that God raised Jesus from the dead.

If you believe that Jesus is living in your heart and Lord of your life, any sin that enters your heart challenges that belief. If you believe Jesus died for your sins, why harbor sin in your heart that will separate you from Him? Noting that both choosing to be unforgiving and choosing to forgive starts in the heart is imperative. Therefore, allow the Word of God to permeate and purify your heart so that everything that is unlike God is purged from it.

Forgiveness becomes easier when you recognize nothing and no one is more important than your relationship with God. Forgiveness is not about the person; it is about you. When you decide that you want the privilege of a relationship with our Creator more than you want the right to be upset with His creation, you will say like Paul in Romans 8:35, "WHO SHALL SEPARATE US [ME] FROM THE LOVE OF CHRIST?..." Then you will answer like he did and say, *"For I am sure that neither death nor life, nor angels nor rulers, nor things present nor things to come, nor powers, nor height nor depth, nor anything else in all creation, will be able to separate us from the love of God in Christ Jesus our Lord"* (ESV).

About 8 years ago, the Lord told me to go on a 40-day fast, so I obeyed. While I was on this fast, God showed me the face of a woman who had offended me by touching me inappropriately as a child. I was only five years old when she molested me. Although it only happened one time, I never forgot what she did nor did I ever forgive her. God wanted me to deal with this unforgiveness. He showed me an emotional trigger that was left after what was done to me. He showed me the root cause of a stronghold that was in my life many years after what happened.

I asked God to remove the anger I held toward this woman and said aloud, "God, if You can forgive me for my sins, I can forgive her." Then, I began to pray for her because the Lord had showed me her behavior was the result of a pattern of perversion. I began to ask God to break strongholds in her family. Finally, I was free from that past offense.

But wait...Are you? The Lord told me when I was writing this part that some who read about my experience will have some uneasy memories triggered or even experience flashbacks of what happened in their childhood, adolescence and/or older years. Therefore, I want to address that possibility and guide you in processing the memories with the hope of helping you overcome the offense/s.

If you do not have a pen handy, please get one and come back to this page. I want you to do a short activity that I believe will help you if you open your heart and mind to the possibility that God can heal you once and for all. Okay, do you have your pen yet? If not, you are about to miss what God wants to do in your life. If you do not have access to one, put this book down and come back to it later when you have one. Now I want you to take a deep breath...

Breathe Freely

I invite you to take time to take this short "Breathe Freely" activity by way of the Holy Spirit:

1.   Inhale slowly while saying in your mind, *"I can do all things through Christ..."* then exhale while saying, "who strengthens me." Repeat this Scripture three times with your eyes closed.

2.   How did you feel when it happened?

_____

3.   What bothered you the most about what happened? (It may be your own helplessness, your fear of telling someone, the child that was conceived etc.)

_____

_____

_____

_____

Take a another deep breath.

4.   Does what happened continue to impact you today?

Please answer by circling YES or NO.

5.   If NO, please continue reading after this activity. If YES,

list in what ways (Think about your current relationships, your ability to

trust, your anger toward men/women, etc.) you still feel the impact.

_____

_____

_____

_____

Releasing the Fracture

If the violation is still impacting you unfavorably, it is because

part of what happened was left emotionally unprocessed. Perhaps, the

incident is too violent to consider or too embarrassing to recall.

Whatever the case, it leaves you fractured and prevents you from moving

forward and receiving true fulfillment in your present relationships. It

may not be that the partners you have met are all untrustworthy; it may very well be that your failure to fully process what happened prevents you from trusting.

When I fractured my ankle, the bones did not heal until I consistently attended physical therapy. Likewise, if you want to be free from living with an emotional, physical, mental, or social fracture, you must be willing to attend spiritual therapy regularly. Let God into the fractured place that you cannot bear to address. You do not have to bear it; He will bear it for you. Psalm 55:22 says, *"Cast your burden upon the LORD and He will sustain you; He will never allow the righteous to be shaken."*

When you release your fracture to God, Scripture notes He will sustain you. The word for *sustain* is *kuwl* which means "to take in or to hold."[12] God knows the fracture hurts, which is why He wants to *kuwl* you. He wants to take you in, hold you and make you whole. In essence, God wants you to be fracture free! Therefore, He says to cast or release your burdens upon Him. In fact, He desires you to carry His burden and not your own as burden of the Lord is *"light"* (Matthew 11:30), which means it is bearable. Will you trade your burden for the burden of the Lord today?

For those who are struggling with giving your fracture to God because you blame Him for what happened or wonder why He allowed it, consider this: God is not like man. He does not impose His will on people, nor does He force them to do anything. God is not a dictator; rather, He is love. Since God is love, He cannot kill someone who is getting ready to violate another person because taking the person's life goes against His character—which is love. In essence, God is not a control freak, so He gives human beings free will. They choose their actions based on their heart or carnal desires. Therefore, God is not responsible for the evil acts of people; they are. Unfortunately, men and women misuse free will by imposing harm on others, i.e., rape, molestation, abuse, etc. You can take peace in knowing that God Himself will judge them. You do not need to carry the fractures of resentment, hatred or anger in your heart because doing so will prevent you from receiving wholeness from the Lord.

I want to include the latter part of my story in the hope of offering you the additional benefits in becoming fracture free. After the Lord showed me the face of the woman I initially refused to forgive, I began to study forgiveness. The study helped me to discover how much I really needed to release the fracture. Not too many days later while I was still on that 40-day fast, God allowed me to encounter this same woman at a funeral. I smiled at her and said, "God bless you" and truly meant it. In that moment, I knew I was free and began to praise God. God set me free so that I could testify that forgiveness brings you to a place where offense no longer matters, and the emotional trigger is dismantled.

While bloody on the cross after being beaten, nailed, spat on, mocked, having a crown of thorns painfully thrust into his head, pierced in His side – Jesus cried out to God not to curse them or kill them, but to "FORGIVE THEM." Why? I believe He knew if they were not forgiven, they would not have any part with Him. He was sent to die for the very ones who had nailed Him on the cross. Christ wanted them to be in relationship with Him so badly that He asked God to pardon them while they were *yet* sinning! He simply did not want their sins to separate them from God's love. He knew they needed to be forgiven, and guess what? So do we! If Christ Himself could say "Father, forgive them" after all they did to Him, and God forgave them, who are we to hold anything against anyone?

God wants a relationship with us so badly that He is willing to forgive and forget what we did that separated us in the first place! May we forgive others that we too may be forgiven. Amen.

III - *Sexless*

What Is Abstinence?

By no stretch of the imagination do I think everyone who is

unmarried is abstinent. If that were the case, 2015 statistics would not

have revealed that 1.6 million children in the United States of America

were born to unwed mothers.[13] Evangelicals, Catholics and Jews alike

would agree that we live in a society that has devalued God's structure of

the family. In this millennial era, television shows portray teenage

parents as something that merits praise and rewards; a role that

teenagers should aspire to in the hopes of becoming the next popular

reality TV star.

What a sad chronicle that this nation has fallen so far away from God's original design for His creation. Nonetheless, even in a sin-sick society, everything is determined by an individual's decision. One person decides to stop smoking cigarettes; another decides to start smoking cigarettes. In either case, both will reap the benefits or burdens of their choices. The same holds true in the case of abstinence.

Countless women are unaware of the benefits of abstinence simply because they do not practice it. Some women perceive abstinence as a burden as opposed to a benefit. This mentality often leaves women feeling as if abstinence is something they could never do. The idea that practicing abstinence is impossible keeps many women from even considering, never mind attempting any self-restraint in the matter.

Merriam-Webster defines *abstinence* as "the practice of not doing or having something that is wanted or enjoyable."[14] I personally love this definition because it makes use of the word "practice" which implies that an act is being consistently repeated. The team that practiced one time and won the Super Bowl has never existed. Likewise, if a woman desires to win the "war" against her flesh, she must practice dying daily to her carnal desires. The key is consistent repetition or gaining a momentum while you practice that evolves into a lifestyle.

The more a woman practices abstinence, the more she will perfect dying to her flesh. As she works daily to perfect dying to her flesh, practicing abstinence becomes her life. She thinks, speaks, interacts, and ultimately lives by this personal discipline.

My sincere belief is that a plethora of women do not practice abstinence simply because of negative perspectives that have been passed down or developed. If a woman only sees what she is restricted from doing and fails to see what she is enriched by doing, she will never experience the blessing of abstinence. Abstinence is much more than what you cannot do; practicing it allows you to gain wisdom that is only available from self-denial. Not a great deal is to be learned when you always do what you are accustomed to doing. If you always drive the same way to work every day, you will never find that one store that sells everything you regularly buy at 50 percent off because it requires taking a different way. Abstinence offers women unique blessings that can only be discovered by taking another route.

It is no secret that the Bible repeatedly warns against fornication. 1 Peter 2:11 states, *"Abstain from fleshly lusts,"* 1 Corinthians 6:18 says, *"Flee fornication"* and in 2 Timothy 2:22 the apostle Paul writes to *"Flee also youthful lusts."* Becoming hung up on the fact that those Scriptures and many others tell the reader what not to do is easy. However, I want to encourage you to go a little deeper. Do not get stuck on what you are forbidden to do according to Scripture; instead, take the time to explore why God included this particular practice. Out of all the practices He could have included, why fornication? Why single out the union between two people? Especially when it is a practice that many find pleasurable, is scientifically proven to reduce stress, burns calories and improves health as Sexual Health Expert Dr. Yvonne K Fulbright notes, "Sexually active people take fewer sick days."[15]

So, if sex is all of that, a bag of chips, dip and your favorite soda on the side—why on earth would God forbid it for singles? To some, it may even appear that God does not want what is best for singles. On the contrary, this is precisely why God forbids it. He knows what is best for you, and if you are entangled in fornication (or any sin for that matter), it will separate you from Him. Isaiah 59:2 says, *"But your iniquities have separated between you and your God, and your sins have hid His face from you that He will not hear."*

Sin imposes on our intimacy with God. We cannot be in a right relationship with God and be enslaved to sin at the same time. The Bible says, *"No man can serve two masters, he will love one and hate the other...."* Clearly, you have two choices here. You can either serve God in love or serve your flesh in lust. The Scripture to which I just alluded can be found in its entirety in Matthew 6:24 where it juxtaposes serving God as one's Master or choosing mammon, which is understood to be money, as one's master. Serving money as one's master can equate to serving an idol which is equally as sinful as serving your flesh, which results in the sin of fornication. God forbids this sin and all sin because they take you outside of the will of God.

The great sixteenth-century Protestant reformer, Martin Luther, condemned priestly celibacy as a universal policy. To be clear, priestly celibacy is not abstinence alone. In fact, ordained priests in the Roman Catholic Church take a vow of celibacy that includes abstaining from marriage to devote themselves completely to God and His church. Luther argued that this vow was contrary to the Word of God. He felt strongly that "it violated the freedom of the gospel and made religion a matter of rules, status, orders, and divisions rather than a spontaneous relation to God through Christ."[16] Luther rejected this vow because he believed it made religion more about restrictions rather than relationship with God.

What Luther believed is precisely what can happen when a woman is fixated on what she is forbidden to do. One reason unbelievers miss out on a relationship with God is because they focus on what they cannot do is. Likewise, some women will never experience the benefits of abstinence because they concentrate solely on what they cannot do. Again, we are brought to the reality that our Sovereign God knows what is best for us.

God created you so He knows you better than you know yourself. He knew your desires before you knew them. Therefore, it is not that He restricts you from what you desire but rather that He desires to give you it by divine design. The Bible is clear that if you *"Delight thyself also in the* LORD; [and] *He shall give thee the desires of thine heart"* (Proverbs 37:4). The word *delight* in its original Hebrew form is the word *anag*,[17] which means "to live delicately, to be merry over or to be glad." When you truly become aware of the benefits of the life you live in the Lord, you will be glad! You will find reasons to be merry in the Lord because you are no longer held captive by what you are "forbidden" to do. When you experience unexplainable joy in simply living for God, you know you are delighting yourself in the Lord. At this point, you can wholeheartedly believe God to grant you the desires of your heart. Although, this should not be the reason for your delight, it is certainly a God-given benefit. When you focus on the benefit, it changes your perception about the burden!

What a blessed assurance it is to know that God will gift you with the desires of your heart within the covenant of marriage. God Himself set aside this extraordinary benefit just for you and your future spouse. Why would you want to share something so intimately beneficial with anyone other than who God designed specifically for you? God knows how good, no...how great intimacy between a husband and a wife can be. Intimacy can be so great that God even inspired Paul to write, *"Do not deprive one another sexually—except when you agree for a time to devote yourselves to prayer..."* (1 Corinthians 7:5, HCSB).

Intimacy is so beneficial to married couples that a break from it requires a mutual agreement and sincere dedication to commune with God. If the Bible has requirements to postpone physical intimacy, could it be that there are divine benefits set aside for married intimacy only? Absolutely! Proverbs 18:22 (NKJV) says, *"He who finds a wife finds a good thing and obtains favor from the LORD."* The verse does not say "When a man finds a girlfriend..." or "When a man finds a boo..." On the contrary, when he finds a wife (Side bar: you do not become a wife when you say "I do"; you are already a wife when he finds you!), then he finds favor with God. This is a sacred benefit of marriage! Millions of people in the world are engaging in premarital sex, but they do not have God's favor because

God set aside intimacy within the bonds of marriage.

The Story

At the tender age of 19, not long after accepting my call into ministry, I learned that I had cervical precancerous cells. Every day of my life, I felt depressed and feared that I would die. I did not tell a soul because I did not want anyone to worry. I continued to see the doctor regularly only to receive even more disheartening news.

During this time, I prayed, asking God for healing, seemingly to no avail. One day, during a follow-up doctor's appointment, she suggested that I undergo surgery to remove the precancerous cells. I do not recall my exact response to the doctor; I only remember crying hysterically while walking to my car. When I sat in the driver's seat, I cried until my insides were shaking. I screamed to God in distress, practically begging for healing. Once I got home on that cold day in December, I stood in the shower, crying out to God and saying "I do not want man to get the glory out of this, so heal me, and I will tell anyone who will listen that You are able."

God spoke to me and said, "I have not healed you because you are praying in fear, doubt and unbelief. I do not move in fear doubt or unbelief."

So, I began to bind fear, doubt, and unbelief, and then I stepped out of the shower still crying out to God for healing. I went into my room with tears in my eyes, took my right hand filled with anointing oil and placed it over my cervix and began to pray earnestly. I felt heat over my cervix, and I began to scream, "Thank You, Jesus!" because I knew it was the Holy Spirit. I had never felt such a supernatural heat in my life. I literally felt something leave my body, and I knew I had been healed.

A few days later, I opened my Bible, and this Scripture seemingly jumped off the page:

> "Forasmuch then as Christ hath suffered for us in the flesh, arm yourselves likewise with the same mind: for he that hath suffered in the flesh hath ceased from sin; That he no longer should live the rest of his time in the flesh to the lusts of men, but to the will of God" (1 Peter 4:1, 2).

This Scripture led me to a life of abstinence. I knew that I could no longer live how my flesh desired. If I were going to "arm (myself) likewise with the same mind" as Christ Himself, I knew I had to change.

I remember thinking to myself about the sufferings of Jesus, which brought about thoughts of my own sufferings. I remembered suffering silently for two years, thinking I would die of cancer; I knew the time had come to "cease from sin" as the Scripture declares. I lost the desire to live according to self-will and gained the desire to live in the will of God. God cared enough about me to allow the sickness, just so He could heal me and bring me to a place of deliverance. What in your life is God allowing to happen to bring you to your place of breakthrough?

About a week later, I had a pre-surgical follow-up appointment. The doctor took some images and came into the room, appearing baffled. She said, "The last time you were here, the cells had gotten bigger. This time I do not see one cell."

"I know, God healed me," I explained.

She simply smiled while still appearing confused. Whether she believed or not, I knew what I had experienced. God performed a miracle on my behalf. To God be all the glory!

The Real

Generally, when a man and a woman become intimate, a sense of attachment forms. I am not referring only to a physical attachment but to a much deeper bond being formed that is spiritual. Under the governance

of marriage, a husband and wife are joined together in a God-honored

soul tie. Ephesians 5:31 states, *"For this cause shall a man leave his father*

and mother, and shall be joined unto his wife, and they two shall be one flesh."

A husband and a wife whom God has joined develop a bond so

deep that scripture describes it as *strong, permanent, and even*

unbreakable by man (Mark 10:7-9). On the other hand, when an

unmarried couple engages in sexual relations, an ungodly soul tie

is formed.

Okay, this next paragraph is about to get real, so I hope you

have fastened your seatbelt. Be mindful, the "medicine" I am about

to dispense to you, I must also consume myself. This medicine is

more than a treatment; it is a cure: Stop confusing a *soul tie* for a

soul mate! Falling prey to this ideal is one of the biggest mistakes'

women make.

A *soul tie* is one that is created based on a person's own

fleshly desires; a soul mate is one God has designed specifically for

an individual. The apostle Paul said in 1 Corinthians 6:16, *"Or do you*

not know that he who is joined to a harlot is one body with her? For the two,

shall become one flesh." In essence, a soul tie can be formed outside of marriage, but it is indeed outside of the will of God. How does one determine a soul tie to be outside of the will of God? Well, God gives us a glimpse into His will in 2 Peter 3:9 where He wills *"...that none would perish but that all would come to repentance."* So, it is safe to say anything that could lead one to perish would be outside of the will of God.

The Bible is clear that sin causes us to perish based on Romans 6:23a, which states, *"The wages of sin is death"*—meaning you perish not only physically but spiritually, mentally and emotionally when you create a soul tie outside of the will of God. The next part of that same Scripture gives us assurance that we will not perish if we accept the gift of God which is eternal life through Jesus Christ our Lord. Jesus died *for* our sins, so that we would not have to die *in* our sins.

If you are struggling with fornicating and really want God to help you break a soul tie/s, study, memorize and declare the following Scriptures out loud until they take root in your heart and you see a change. If Christ can raise the dead, heal the sick, give sight to the blind and hearing to the deaf, then certainly He can break a soul tie! He will break the soul tie in your life *if* you allow Him to.

When you reach the point where you desire God more than fornication, that is when the soul tie breaks. Never in a million years would I have thought or dreamed that many years after God delivered me, He would instruct me to write a book on the subject. What God will do in your life when you really let Jesus into your heart is unimaginable! Believe me, change is possible with Christ in your heart and applying the Word of God to your life. Only believe!

The following Scriptures will help you start on your journey toward freedom:

1 Corinthians 10:13, *"There hath no temptation taken you but such as is common to man: but God is faithful, who will not suffer you to be tempted above that ye are able; but will with the temptation also make a way to escape, that ye may be able to bear it."*

Hebrews 12:1 (ESV), *"Therefore, since we are surrounded by so great a cloud of witnesses, let us also lay aside every weight, and sin* *which clings so closely, and let us run with endurance the race that is set before us."*

2 Corinthians 10:5, *"Casting down imaginations, and every high thing that exalteth itself against the knowledge of God, and bringing into captivity every thought to the obedience of Christ."*

When I decided to live a life of abstinence, I had no idea the amount of benefits that would accompany that decision. Although, there are a great deal more, I have chosen to include my top seven below:

7 Lessons Learned from Living God's Way

#1 God is priority.

Abstinence allows you to put aside your fleshly desires and seek God above all. By turning your affections towards the Lord, you can develop a stronger prayer life, a consistent fasting life and an overall better relationship with Him. Matthew 6:33 says, *"But seek ye first the kingdom of God, and his righteousness; and all these things shall be added unto you."* This verse contains the secret to receiving everything you need in this life: maintain God's order of priorities. When you are kingdom conscious, God is first thus making the things of God primary.

The actions of a single sister who is kingdom conscious reveal she is not distracted by where she is but astounded by where she is going. Her mind is focused on Heaven or the things of God which means she is not consumed by the things of this world. If the things of God are most important, then the things of this world, such as loneliness or rejection become less important. In essence, they lose the power to overcome you. Our kingdom mindset assures us that God will never leave us nor forsake us. Often, *righteousness* or being in right standing with God is neglected because so many other people and things steal our attention. The more you put God first, the more He has your undivided attention. This means, the more He has your attention, the more you have His attention. Therefore, that which you need or desire from the Lord is yours for the asking.

If you are struggling with allowing God to take precedence above all others this verse is for you:

> 1 Corinthians 7:34, *"The unmarried woman careth for the things of the Lord, that she may be holy both in body and in spirit: but she that is married careth for the things of the world, how she may please her husband."*

Focus on caring for "the things of the Lord" for in doing so you may be "holy in body and in spirit." Having a God-first life becomes less complicated when you set your affections on what God cares about. What is it that God wants you to care about? Single sisters, God does not want you to be so concerned about who your husband is and the ways that you will please him. Based on the above noted scripture from 1 Corinthians, those are things that married woman should be concerned about.

Perhaps some of us are still undesirably unmarried because we are stuck on caring about a husband who has not yet found us rather than the things of God. Take time to pray and ask God to help you be concerned about His concerns. I have heard many married women say that when their husbands found them, they were no longer overly concerned about marriage. I strongly believe when you set your affections on God, He will give you a husband who has done the same. This way the both of you would have already recognized God as the foundation for your life singularly. Therefore, when the two of you come together, you can build off an already established God-centered foundation.

If you desire to begin or continue a life of abstinence, I will not pretend making that decision is easy. However, I do attest to the fact that adhering to the choice becomes less challenging over time with the help of the Lord. Submitting yourself to God, resisting the Devil and watching him flee is a daily effort. With the Holy Spirit's help, living a sexless life is not impossible.

#2 Keep the temple clean.

One day, I was walking in a building and admiring how beautiful it was. The building's spaciousness, bright colors and architectural features looked as if it should have been displayed on the pages of a fancy magazine. As I walked up its spiral staircase, I took my time to observe the plethora of details. When I got to the second level, I exited the staircase and walked inside the first room I saw. To my surprise, there was dust coating the room! It was so prevalent; I could not lie my coat down anywhere in the room. You would have thought with all the bells and whistles of the building, the least someone could have done was dust!

This building mirrors precisely what can happen in the life of single sister who is abstinent. You can become so used to appearing abstinent externally that you no longer take time to dust internally. 1 Corinthians 6:4 refers to your body as a temple of the Holy Spirit. This means, if you are a believer in Christ, His Spirit resides within you. Would you want the place where God dwells to be left unkept? A lack of proper cleaning or dusting will result in buildup. However, dusting properly will result in growth. Simply put, the only way to keep ones temple clean is to wash in the Word of God daily. You might think that simply utilizing your willpower will suffice, but it is not more powerful than the fruit of self-control given to you by Gods Spirit. Now, the Holy Spirit Himself works in you to produce self-control (Galatians 5:22-23), which is what makes it more powerful than anything your flesh can offer. The way to keep your temple clean is to allow the Holy Spirit to produce more fruit in your life. By washing in the Word daily, the fruit will become more and more evident. Do not become comfortable because you are not fornicating. Do not think you can resist temptation without the fruit of self-control and the Word of God. You must eat, drink, and meditate on the Word of God in order to be free and **stay free**.

Many people receive deliverance, but they do not all remain delivered because they do not practice what brought them to the place of deliverance in the first place. I have already shared that God's word has enables me to live a sexless life until marriage. Since the Word of God is what propelled me to live this life, only the Word of God will be able to sustain me.

I encourage you, if you have never opened a Bible and desire to live a life of abstinence, open it now! Begin to study, find a Bible study group, a Bible-teaching church, etc. Allow God to take full residence in your temple. Your temple is valuable; it is worth something to God. After all, it was made in His image and likeness. Why not allow the One who made you to dwell within you? His presence within your body purifies you and makes you whole. The presence of God can purify that carnal longing for sex and lead you to realize you are not missing out. In fact, physical intimacy between a man and a woman can not compare to spiritual intimacy with the Father. There is no greater intimacy than that of the Father. Spending time with Him will purify your heart, mind and body in ways you never knew you needed.

#3 Balance, but do not compromise.

2 Corinthians 6:14 says, *"Be ye not unequally yoked together with unbelievers: for what fellowship hath righteousness with unrighteousness? And what communion hath light with darkness?"*

Balance is not compromise, and compromise is not balance. In terms of living a Christian life of holiness, balance is important. You do not want to become dogmatic nor ritualistic in your walk with the Lord. You are no longer under the Old Testament Law; now that Christ has fulfilled it, therefore you may live freely. Living freely does not mean doing whatever your flesh desires; rather, it means finding balance between what God requires of you and what He has entrusted you to have stewardship over in your life. Be sure to give ample time to the things of God while not neglecting family, friends, and pastimes. Incorporating balance in a sexless life can be of much benefit.

Some complain that they cannot live the Christian life of abstinence because it is boring. However, anything you continuously repeat without a break in between can become boring. If you only go to church, church events or Bible study and fail to incorporate any means of extracurricular activities, you can easily become "churched-out," which is a polite way of saying *bored*.

God does not want His children to be bored because boredom eventually leads to compromise and even burnout. To be clear, compromise is any sinful act that you engage in which causes you to stray away from the plan and purpose of God for your life. Making time for clean fun such as games with friends, taking vacations, playing sports, watching a movie with family, or going to the park alone to clear mental space is crucial for those who desire to live a sexless life. Establishing balance between your spiritual life and your natural life will help you to avoid compromise. It is my belief that some single women compromise their morals, values and even standards when they fail to establish balance. Whether it is work-life balance or life-church balance, finding a healthy common ground for all aspects of your life will decrease the likelihood of backsliding. Consider this: Being in a church building did not dictate whether or not Jesus lived upright. It also did not determine whether he ministered effectively or not. In fact, Scripture captured Jesus ministering mostly outside of church walls. In fact, He was seen enjoying festivals, visiting friends and even dining with sinners. If Jesus made time for extracurricular activities, how much more should we as His followers do the same?

#4 Prepare, prepare, prepare.

Anyone who knows me well, knows that I do not entertain "feel good" or prosperity preaching. I prefer messages that call my flesh into subjection and challenge me to pursue Gods plan for my life. With that in mind, one day I received a prophetic word from a visiting Pastor that God was going to heal my heart of guilt (tied to my ex) that I carried for several years. As she prophesied to me, it felt as though I could feel the guilt breaking off my heart which brought me to tears. Then, the Pastor told me to "let it go" and that my husband was coming. The presence of the Lord was so strong all over me in that moment that all I could do was praise God while tears rolled down my face.

What amazed me was, that very same week, I had said to the Lord that if He wanted me to be single, I wanted His will for my life above all else—though singleness was not my desire, I would accept it if it was His will. So, there was no doubt in my mind that this was a true word from the Lord. I love the fact that God can speak to us in ways that do not fit our expectations, which assures me that He is not constricted to our finite preferences. Thank God! He will speak how He wants whenever He wants. Our responsibility is to be prepared to hear and receive our *"Thus saith the Lord..."*

After this prophetic word was released, I felt as if every wrong man on the planet also received a notification. I literally was sought after by seven to eight different men within the course of four months. Never in my life have that many men expressed interest in me all at once. I knew the Enemy was sending counterfeits because of the prophetic word had been released. I prayed and asked the Lord to give me discernment and help me not to be carnal in my choice of men.

I encourage every woman to do exactly that. When you find yourself inundated with a ton of "Mr. Wrongs," ask God to give or increase your spiritual discernment that you will be able to identify who (if any) are God's choice. *Discern* or *ra'ah* in the Greek simply means "to see."[17] When God gives you discernment, you will see beyond how handsome or attractive he may be in the natural. Discernment will tell you that an attractive man without God in His heart is not attractive at all.

On another note, unless you want to be single, sexy, and sexless for the rest of your life, I suggest you prepare yourself for marriage. Planning a wedding and planning a marriage are two different *animals*. Too often women are not clear on which one they desire most. Many women get the itch for a wedding but have no sense of urgency about preparing for a marriage.

Listen, my sister, if this description fits you: buy yourself a white dress, throw yourself a party and pretend to be the bride for the day. Seriously! Too many women envision a beautiful, fairytale-like wedding but fail to envision a successful marriage. With this being stated, I ask which do you want? Anyone can have a gorgeous wedding that is talked about for years after the celebration is over, but not everyone can have a successful marriage.

If you want to have a successful marriage, you should be proactive. If you are praying for a husband, **prepare for what you have prayed for!** Perhaps God has not allowed your husband to find you because you are not prepared. If you are a single, courting or an engaged woman who desires marriage, have you prepared? If not, you should not expect to be a great wife, have a great husband, or ultimately have a great marriage.

As a single woman, you must prepare your mind, body, and spirit to be a wife. Mentally, you cannot afford to carry the girlfriend mentality into a marriage and expect it to work. If you are going to shift out of the mentality of a girlfriend (no binding commitment is required) to the mentality of a wife (a binding commitment *is* required), you must be willing to learn. Do not only consult those who are married but be sure to consult those who are happily married in God. Godly counsel or *"the mouth of the righteous"* as the Bible declares in Psalm 37:30, *"speaks wisdom."* Stay away from those who are inexperienced in marriage for counsel unless you believe they have the gift of wisdom.

Besides seeking and receiving godly counsel, you should study, study, study! Hosea 4:6 says, *"My people are destroyed for lack of knowledge...."* Without proper or adequate knowledge, God's people are destroyed. If you are destroyed, what do you think will happen to your marriage? Study what the Biblical role of a wife should be according to the New Testament, which shares ample amounts of sound instruction to help women understand their role as wives.

Some things, of course, will be on-the-job training in a new marriage, but imagine how many marriages would be better (or even saved from divorce court) if they knew what God had to say about it beforehand. The following is a brief list of some foundational Scriptures to use for your study: Titus 2:4-5, 1 Peter 3:1, 1 Timothy 3:11, and Ephesians 5:22-24.

#5 Use your time wisely.

Single women, a life of sexlessness enables you to develop self-discipline. That discipline should spill over into other areas of your life. When this happens, you will have something to bring to the table besides a nice smile and/or body. In the time that you are afforded in your singleness, maximize every moment you have. Going after your dreams, aspirations and goals is great; however, while you are chasing them, save your money, learn about investments, open a business, etc. Do not put a man in a position that makes him feel like you are a burden rather than a blessing.

If you use every moment wisely, your future husband will not see you as someone who is looking for a handout. Use the time God has gifted you with to become proactive. You have so much more time now to build and establish than you ever will once you are married with children. I am not saying it is impossible but I am saying it is more challenging when you have additional responsibilities.

Again, make time for prayer so you are clear on what it is God has ordained for your life. I want to emphasize that you should pursue your goals **after** seeking God on what your goals should be. Do this with the intent of uncovering whether or not they are of Him. Proverbs 19:21 says, *"Many are the plans in a person's heart, but it is the Lord's purpose that prevails."* So do not sit around on the couch of singleness, twiddling your fingers and doing nothing. Start to gain and maintain momentum. Get your credit in order, see a credit specialist if necessary, find a mental health therapist to address over your past hurts, pay off your student loans, etc. Do something that will benefit the future you which for many of us is—the married you.

Getting into a marriage with an enormous amount of debt makes absolutely no sense! Especially when you have had ample time to resolve it or at least set an action plan to do so. In the United States, being completely debt-free can be challenging; however, single people have an advantage to paying off their bills because they are the only ones for whom they are financially responsible.

Some single women sit around waiting for a man to come rescue them when it would behoove them to use their time wisely. What if

Peter Pan never comes? Or what if he does come and sees you as a leech? A wife should not be a leech; a wife should be a helpmeet! She should be there to help with whatever the husband wants to do, build or create. If you have no expertise in any area because you spent many years being lazy and single rather than productive and single, then you cannot help him. So, if you cannot help, how can you be effective as a wife?

I believe "a helpless helpmeet" is an oxymoron. If you are a helpmeet, then you should be helpful. If you are not a helpmeet, then you will be helpless. **If you are helpless, you are not helpmeet material.**

If you expect God to send your husband who you are not prepared to help and have a successful marriage, you have false expectations. Perhaps your lack of proper preparation is why your husband has not found you. Prepare yourself to help by getting yourself help-ready! Become consistent about getting in shape. I am not saying be skinny; I am saying be healthy—physically, emotionally, spiritually, financially, and even socially.

Try maximizing your life in such a way that when the husband God created for you finds you, he finds you ready! No husband is looking for a waiting mess; therefore, be a waiting wife. Use your time or you will lose your time. Years can go by within a blink of an eye, and you will feel like there is so much more that you could have accomplished. Perhaps you feel like this now, but it is never too late. Never mind where you are now or how much time has gone by. You can take charge now by beginning to do something different than you have done in the past. What sense is there in saying, "I could have, would have or should have," rather than saying, "I am starting today!" Perhaps you have not realized how much time you have been wasting in your single life but let this portion of the book motivate you to use your time wisely. So, what better time is there to start than now?

#6 Learn how to fight.

The bottom line is not every day in the life of one who is sexless is easy. To the contrary, some days can be exceedingly difficult because your flesh wants what it wants, which is to rebel against God. So how does a single woman overcome the temptations of the flesh? Again, the only way the temptations of the flesh can be overcome is through the Word of God. Read, study and apply the Word of God in every situation for it is the only means of victory for the believer.

You learn how to fight by rendering yourself over to God. Without submitting yourself to God, you will think that you can win the battle against your flesh in your own strength. Remember, the battle is not yours; it belongs to the Lord (2 Chronicles 2:15). Sure, some individuals who live a life of abstinence are not Christian nor do they identify with any particular faith tradition or religion. However, they are submitted to their own self-will, which is contrary to the life of the believer. Our self-will dies when we submit ourselves to God. If you want to live out this Christian life, we must be holy as He is holy. Therefore, submit your whole self over to the Lord. Your flesh is not stronger than God!

Many get caught up in the latter part of Matthew 26:41 that says, *"...the flesh is weak."* Some even use this phrase to justify their sins. However, the cure for the weakness of the flesh is found in this segment the verse: *"...the spirit is willing...."* Be mindful that when your flesh is at its weakest point, your spirit-man who is subject to the Holy Spirit is still willing. If you begin to avail your ear to what your spirit-man is saying in those moments of temptation such as "take the way of escape," you will overcome the temptation of the flesh.

Someone may be pondering, what if it is not my flesh? Or what if it is the Devil? To this point, the believer must know his or her authority. One of my favorite scriptures is Luke 10:19, which says, *"Behold, I give unto you power to tread on serpents and scorpions and all power of the enemy and nothing shall by any means harm you."* As a believer, you have been given authority over poisonous, harmful, and even lethal natural and spiritual beings that would otherwise destroy you. This authority includes all power of the Enemy, which includes every power, principality, spiritual wickedness, generational curses, witchcraft, and any other form of Satanic opposition. You have power over it because Christ has given it to you. Whether or not you utilize His power is up to you.

This goes hand in hand with submitting to God as this is how you resist satanic temptation. Once you resist him, he must flee from you. James 4:7 says, *"Submit yourself therefore to God. Resist the devil, and he will flee from you."* If you are going to live a life of abstinence, you must be willing to let go of your own desires and submit every part of your person unto God. Mind, body, spirit, and soul must all be surrendered unto God.

The Adversary cannot reside in a space that is filled by God. If you have filled your mind, heart and body with the Word of God, the Enemy cannot infiltrate those areas. The word *submit* in James 4:7 in its original Greek form means "subordinate, to arrange under, to be subject to or to obey."[18] **When you have submitted your whole self to the Lord, the Enemy cannot successfully tempt you to sin.**

So, my friend, what are you waiting for? If you are tired of falling for the traps and snares of the Enemy, SUBMIT! Once you submit to

God, you become more aware of the devices of the Enemy and more skilled in using your authority to overcome them. Although every temptation is not the Devil, it is important that you remember to always be on guard. For those who may be wondering "Why do I need to be on guard?" simply put, evil *is* present (Romans 7:21). Evil can and will present itself at the most inopportune times, and often when you are lulled into a series of distractions which I shared more deeply about in my first book, *Birthing Purpose Against All Odds*. However, when you realize you have authority over evil, you will know that God is *always* present. Being that God is always present, you can always use your God-given authority over all present evil.

#7 Work while you wait.

For a drug user to stop using drugs in isolation is hard; when he or she is constantly surrounded by other drug users, to stop using is even harder. This same principle can be applied for this seventh and final lesson. If you constantly surround yourself with "project people" meaning people who always need you to fix them, their problem or their dilemma, you will never have time to work on you. How can you be completely effective in helping someone else become healthy if you are not healthy yourself? Think about it. Would you trust a person who says,

"I have never before been skydiving, but I am going to be your trainer for your first jump?"

No, absolutely not, right? How ridiculous! What possible help is this person who has never taken time to learn the art of skydiving? You run the risk of dying by placing your life in the hands of one who is untrained to protect it. You and anyone else with any ounce of intelligence would all desire an expert in the field. You want someone who took time to work on their craft and can ensure your safety.

This same principle of working must be applied in the lives of single women. Any expert you meet in life did not wake up one day, and *voilà*, he or she is now an expert! Neither will you drink a magic potion and become an expert either. Each day you should work toward becoming who God has created you to be. Work to walk into the purpose God has predestined over your life. Do not become comfortable working a 9am-5pm when you know God has gifted you to become an entrepreneur. Do not do what is most comfortable, but work to learn new information, crafts and skills.

On a personal note, I must admit that I am guilty of being an overachiever. I have a habit of multitasking, which keeps me terribly busy all year round. I take on multiple projects, am constantly in pursuit of a new goal and have a daily to-do list. So, I sometimes do not even consider the fact that I am single because I am too busy being busy. Over the course of my single life journey, I have been inundated with attaining degrees, securing a career, working out, writing books, planning events, ministering, coordinating ministry engagements and building a business among other ventures. The point is, I actually became so busy that it was not until my best friend said to me, "I want to go to your wedding and be there when you have your first baby already," that I remembered I want those things too. Being busy working to secure my future kept me from focusing on being single. However, taught me something powerful. Filling space with achieving goals does not equate to working on yourself in your singleness. Work on YOU!

I have met several women who have become bitter, hopeless and frustrated in their singleness because they are preoccupied with the thought of being married. Some want to be married so badly that they fail to take advantage of their singleness. Waiting on "the one" can become draining if it becomes an obsession or a person's sole aspiration. So, avoid waiting in vain by taking the time to focus on your career, build up your spiritual life, find a new hobby, finish school, join the gym, write the book, etc. In essence, make time to work on you and ensure that anyone who you allow to come into your space respects that time.

Takeaways

Congratulations! You made it to the end of the book. But wait...this is not the end by any means; this is your beginning. Now that you have learned about being single, sexy, and sexless, what are you going to do with what you have learned? Please take a moment to complete the following short activity. Be sure to interact with the section that most honestly describes you.

Single and Sexless
1. What was your biggest takeaway?

_____

_____

_____

2. Why do you think that thought or principle stood out the most?

_____

_____

_____

3. How can you apply what you have learned in your daily life?

_____

_____

_____

_____

4. When will you apply this truth? **(Be specific.)** *Remember, if you fail to plan, you plan to fail.*

_____

_____

_____

Single and Sexually Active

1. What was your biggest takeaway?

_____

_____

_____

Would you like to practice abstinence? If YES, go to **2A**. If NO, go to **2B**.
2A. YOU CAN DO IT through Christ who strengthens you! You must believe you can! Mark 9:23 tells us that all things are possible for him (or her) that believes. First, believe that you can and submit yourself to God. Second, believe that you can resist temptation whether it be Satanic or your own fleshly desires. Maintain a consistent prayer, study and fasting life. Doing so will encourage the continual dying of the flesh, thus making it harder to fall into temptation. These are some key practices that will enable you to live a life of abstinence until God sends your mate (if that is your desire.)

2B. Thank you for being honest. No judgment. We all have our own paths to take and lessons to learn. Know that if you change your mind and dare to try something different than what you are used to, you will reap endless benefits. Whenever you choose God's way, the benefits are as limitless as He is. Continue to pray and ask God to guide you in your decisions and desires. Trust Him for what you do not understand and believe Him for what you cannot see. Remember, *"Now faith is the substance of things hoped for, the evidence of things not seen"* (Hebrews 11:1). Only believe!

3. How can you apply what you have learned in your daily life?

_____

_____

_____

4. When will you apply it? *(Be specific.)* Remember, if you fail to plan, you plan to fail.

_____

_____

_____

Best Part

If you would like to receive Jesus Christ as your personal Lord and Savior, today is your day! God is giving you the opportunity today to receive Him into your heart. Will you accept it? God loves you so much that He does not want you to deal with temptation, sin, perversion, fetishes, fantasies (or whatever it is) on your own. John 3:16, the greatest love story ever told, says *"For God so loved the world that He gave His only begotten Son, that whosoever believes in Him should not perish but have everlasting life."* I admonish you to receive Jesus into your heart and allow Him to help you say "no" to a life of sin and "yes" to external life with Him. Romans 10:9-10 makes clear when a person believes in their heart and confesses with their mouth that God raised Jesus from the dead then he or she is saved. If you believe, please recite aloud the following prayer to accept Jesus today:

Lord Jesus,

I come to you confessing and repenting of all of my sins and asking You to forgive me. I believe You died, shed Your precious blood and rose from the dead for me. Come into my heart and fill me with Your Holy Spirit. Today I receive You into my heart as my personal Lord and Savior. Reveal Yourself to me and help me to acknowledge You in all my ways so You may direct my path. Thank You for forgiving me and saving me. In Jesus' name, Amen.

If you prayed the above prayer, CONGRATULATIONS! Today, you became a member of the body of Christ! You are now saved from eternal damnation and a recipient of eternal life. This means when you leave this Earth, you will enter the kingdom of God forever. Heaven is throwing a party right now because you just received Jesus as your Lord and Savior. God loves you, keep growing in love with Him.

About the Author

Daphne R Beard is a NYS Board Certified Chaplain who offers spiritual and emotional support to persons of all faiths in a nationally ranked medical center. She is certain that her calling is not limited to a specific people group but fervently believes the anointing of God surpasses all racial, religious and gender boundaries. Her areas of specialty include but are not limited to end of life care, bereavement support, crisis situations etc.

She is licensed and ordained to preach the Gospel of Jesus Christ and serves in a local Christian church. She received her Bachelor of Arts Degree in Biblical and Theological Studies from Nyack College in Manhattan, New York and her Master of Divinity Degree in Chaplaincy from Liberty University Baptist Theological Seminary in Lynchburg, Virginia. She is currently pursuing her Doctorate degree in Theology at Trinity Theological Seminary in Evansville, Indiana. To God be all of the glory!

Acknowledgements

To the best mother a girl could ask for, you have shown me what it means to live the life you believe. Thank you for walking in integrity before God and man. Words could never express how grateful I am to be your daughter. The older I become, the more grateful I am to have a mother who is an example of what it means to be a woman of faith. I love you far beyond words and thank you for loving me!

To my "siblingers," I thank God for you two – you make being a big sister worth it! I pray you continue to pursue your dreams and never stop growing in God. Live life without limits as there are no limitations in Him. I am proud of both of you and love you two so very much!

To the most incredible photographer/videographer, Vinson McCrea of IHL Media in Orange, NJ. Thank you for your keen eye and great patience in working to perfect each image, video, and all promotional needs for this project. Thank you for bringing my vision to life and helping to make this project a success.

To the most gracious editor, Linda Stubblefield of Affordable Christian Editing in Merrillville, IN. Your decades of editing experience and teaching in seminary are evident in your work on this project. Thank you for your words of wisdom, encouragement and carrying everything out with the spirit of excellence.

End Notes

[1] Tamra Ryan, *The Third Law*. Denver, CO: Gilpin House Press, 2013.

[2] "Simplicity." Accessed August 11, 2018. https://www.merriam-webster.com/dictionary/simplicity

[3] Bratt Pitt, Dede Gardner, and Jeremy Kleiner, *Eat Pray Love,* [DVD], Directed by Ryan Murphy, Culver City, Calif.: Columbia Pictures, 2010.

[4] Theresa E. DiDonato, "*5 Ways to Heal a Broken Heart,*" *Psychology Today*. Assessed January 04, 2018. http://www.psychologytoday.com/blog/meet-catch-and-keep/201504/5-ways-heal-broken-heart.

[6] James Strong, The New Strong's Exhaustive Concordance of the Bible: with Main Concordance, Appendix to the Main Concordance, Topical Index to the Bible, Dictionary of the Hebrew Bible, Dictionary of the Greek Testament. Nashville, TN: T. Nelson Publishers, 1996.

[7] "Sexy." Accessed August 11, 2018. https://www.merriam-webster.com/dictionary/sexy

[8] James Strong, The New Strong's Exhaustive Concordance of the Bible: with Main Concordance, Appendix to the Main Concordance, Topical Index to the Bible, Dictionary of the Hebrew Bible, Dictionary of the Greek Testament. Nashville, TN: T. Nelson Publishers, 1996.

[9] BLS Reports, "Women in the Labor Force: A Databook," February 2013. https://www.bls.gov/cps/wlf-databook-2012.pdf

[10] Center for Disease Control and Prevention, "Sexual Violence Is Preventable," Accessed May 1, 2019. https://www.cdc.gov/injury/features/sexual-violence.

[11] "Childhood Domestic Violence." Accessed February 11, 2018. https://cdv.org/2014/02/10-startling-domestic-violence-statistics-for-children/.

[12] James Strong, The New Strong's Exhaustive Concordance of the Bible: with Main Concordance, Appendix to the Main Concordance, Topical Index to the Bible, Dictionary of the Hebrew Bible, Dictionary of the Greek Testament. Nashville, TN: T. Nelson Publishers, 1996.

[13] "FastStats - Unmarried Childbearing," Accessed December 9, 2019. https://www.cdc.gov/nchs/fastats/unmarried-childbearing.htm.

[14] "Abstinence." Accessed August 11, 2018. https://www.merriam-webster.com/dictionary/abstinence

[15] Kara Mayer Robinson, "10 Surprising Health Benefits of Sex," October 24, 2013. https://www.webmd.com/sex-relationships/guide/sex-and-health.

[16] Carl Olson, *Celibacy and Religious Traditions*. Oxford: Oxford University Press, 2008.

[17] James Strong, The New Strong's Exhaustive Concordance of the Bible: with Main Concordance, Appendix to the Main Concordance, Topical Index to the Bible, Dictionary of the Hebrew Bible, Dictionary of the Greek Testament. Nashville, TN: T. Nelson Publishers, 1996.

[18] Ibid.

www.ingramcontent.com/pod-product-compliance
Lightning Source LLC
Chambersburg PA
CBHW020906100426
42737CB00044B/546